AS I SEEM TO REMEMBER

SIR LEONARD WOOLLEY

F.S.A.

As I Seem to Remember

ILLUSTRATIONS BY SPROD

LONDON

GEORGE ALLEN AND UNWIN LTD

on behalf of

SHAFTESBURY AND DISTRICT SOCIETY AND MUSEUM

FIRST PUBLISHED IN 1962

© George Allen & Unwin Ltd, 1962

PRINTED IN GREAT BRITAIN
in 10 point Juliana type
BY THE BLACKFRIARS PRESS LTD
LEICESTER

Sir Leonard Woolley, D.Litt., Ll.D., F.S.A., A.R.I.B.A., archaeologist and author, is well assured of his niche in the Temple of Fame. But Leonard Woolley, the man, with his rich store of humanity and humour, his face crinkling with fun as he recalled amusing episodes in his career, is only too likely to be lost to sight.

Sir Leonard Woolley and I knew each other for longer than he knew anyone outside his own family—off and on, but chiefly off, since his professional life, including two years imprisonment in Turkey during the Kaiser's War, took him away so far and so long that big gaps occurred. We first met as fellow navvies, but under different foremen, on the Corbridge Roman excavation. It was his very first dig and, being Victorians, we were still living and working in an era of pick and shovel technique and would today have been dubbed 'Potato Diggers'. At first, and never since, I had the advantage of him, as I had already been a workman in a quarry gang for two years. Perhaps that was why he became known at Corbridge as 'The Gent' while I, having fallen into a dirty ditch on my arrival, was 'Mucky Lad' and 'Mucky' for short.

We paid little attention to each other then, having no idea of what important people we were to become! We did not meet again for many years, when I took the Chair for him at Cambridge at his very first lecture. He was already a marked man and was recognised as such. But I was still 'Mucky'.

Later our friendship was renewed, when he was living at Sedgehill, a few miles from Shaftesbury, where I had recently settled. I had been instrumental in founding the Shaftesbury and District History Society and Museum in 1946 and Sir Leonard took a keen and constant interest in these two institutions. To the Society, of which he became President, he delivered several formal lectures on the subject of his excavations in the East, and four informal talks on his recollections, gay, grave and dramatic. It is the material of these talks which constitutes the bulk of this tribute to his memory. By the courtesy of the B.B.C. we are also able to incorporate the substance of two recorded talks given for the Corporation; these include the episode of the Auction Sale (p. 40), the story of the Kurd who wrote to God (p. 74), and the incident of the Railway Train (p. 43). This last may perhaps strike some readers as trivial; but it serves to illustrate Woolley's readiness to appreciate in others the courtesy which he himself always displayed.

Sir Leonard was completely free from intellectual snobbery. He never talked down to his audience but paid them the compliment of assuming that they were capable of following his lucid exposition of his subject. This attitude of his is well illustrated in the following story which he told himself.

'I remember on one terrible occasion, I was asked to go to a considerable city in the middle-west of America to give a lecture to the senior classes of all the Government Schools in that city; it was to be an Archaeological lecture suited for the upper forms. I went there and got to the Hall, and at the entrance I was met by the lady with whom I had been corresponding on the subject, and to my surprise she was in tears. I said "What is the matter?"

' "Oh!" she said, "a terrible thing has happened!"

' "What is that?"

' "Well," she said, "we asked you to come here and address the upper forms of the Government Schools, but we quite forgot to ask the City Council for permission to get the children here. It was only at the last minute that we asked them, and they took umbrage and they've kept all the children in the schools, and we haven't got an audience for you at all."

'Now, I was supposed to have about 350 senior boys and girls there, so I said "That is very sad", and looked through the curtains at the front of the platform and sure enough there was a very large hall. There were perhaps four people, obviously parents, sitting scattered about in the auditorium, who had meant to meet their children there, but the children hadn't turned up; and in the front row there were five little children, aged I should think eight to eleven, sitting together and waiting for my lecture. As I turned round the unfortunate lady secretary asked me "What on earth are you going to do?"

'I said, "I am going to give my lecture," and she said "You can't, there is nobody to listen".

' "On the contrary," said I, "I have got just the audience that I like", and I proceeded.

'I had a lantern, of course. I told the operator to get to work, and I began to give an hour's lecture on Archaeology to the five small children. I didn't talk down to them at all, I gave a proper adult lecture, which I was sure they would understand and appreciate, and they seemed to—they were rapt. But about three-quarters of the way through, one of them, a little girl aged about ten, started shifting about on her seat and I thought "Hallo, she is getting tired". I looked at her and she realised what was in my mind, and moving to one side, she pointed to the wooden seat of the chair on which she was sitting and said "It is all right, go on".

'I really felt that my audience was a delightful one.'

He was a man of slight stature and no commanding appearance—but presence, yes!—and even a blind man would know what manner of man he was.

And now he has gone, having carefully finished all the work he owed to posterity and therefore to himself, plus a little over for good measure in the form of his share of UNESCO's history of the scientific and cultural development of mankind, which still remains to be published.[1] Really big and responsible men (e.g. Gordon Child) do tend to finish off their work before they die, if chance also favours them.

He was a mighty worker and almost to the end he worked on that last job from about nine in the evening until the early hours of the morning and then, as often as not, would spend the rest of the day trout fishing near here.

He was the very closest and tightest writer for whom I have had to read and yet his work still remained easy to the eye and to the understanding of his readers. In addition to

[1] By George Allen & Unwin in 1962.

his professional abilities he was a very dear person to far more people than most old men could claim to be, and he was as gay as a lark till his final illness.

But his very dearest and, I fancy, his almost revered friend was Hamoudi, his Arab foreman. Read *Dead Towns and Living Men* (Lutterworth Press). That and this small book are perhaps the only publications where Sir Leonard's future biographer may find something of the real man.

Mr L. F. Salzman, C.B.E., who was for fifty years Editor of the *Sussex Archaeological Collections* and for many years Editor of the *Victoria County Histories*, has very generously consented to edit this book. I say generously and not only kindly, for even now he is far from being short of a job. He, too, has been our Society's very good friend ever since our foundation in 1946.

The actual arrangement of the individual talks has not been adhered to, the stories being re-grouped more or less by subjects; but the wording throughout is Woolley's, with only such slight alterations as were necessary to bridge the inevitable gap between the spoken and the printed word. As the essential purpose of these talks was to encourage interest in the Shaftesbury Museum it has seemed suitable to start with a section of anecdotes connected with Museums, but no intending reader need fear that he will be faced with dry and lifeless specimens.

N. TEULON PORTER
Vice-President
Shaftesbury Local History Society

CONTENTS

I

MUSEUM PIECES

Whenever I visit the Shaftesbury Museum I am struck by the extraordinary interest of the place, the way it is arranged, and the way it is labelled, so that it does seem to me a small local Museum qualified to appeal to any intelligent person of almost any age. The mere fact of labelling means so much —I've known museums where there were no labels at all.

Years and years ago when I was quite young I went to see the Roman Museum at Chester, on the Roman Wall. It was in the garden of a private house; as a matter of fact, all the excavations had been carried out virtually in the garden by the gardener. It hadn't been a scientific excavation, but it had been a very long-continued one and very successful; so they built a Museum and put all the stuff there, and as the gardener was beyond work out of doors they made him curator, and he took me round and explained how things had been found, and where, and so on.

We came to a desk-case in which were a number of iron arrowheads, and he pointed to these and said 'Them's arrowheads,' and I said 'Oh yes?'

'Yes' he said. 'You see, them there Romans when they had broken their swords and thrown away their spears, they fell back on these here things.'

I said, 'Yes, I suppose they had to'.

'Yes,' he said. 'You see, Sir, it's an absolute fact, as is scientifically known, that they hadn't got no gunpowder in them days.'

I said, 'No, I believe that's so'.

'Well,' he said, 'that's a fact, sir. And it's my personal belief—I may be mistaken, but I feel fairly sure, Sir,—that they hadn't got no guns either!'

The labelling of things in a Museum is essential, but it is not so simple as might be supposed. Only too often the Director of a Museum, having a great deal of knowledge

They hadn't got no gunpowder

himself, doesn't realise that that knowledge is not necessarily common property, and he does not take, therefore, into consideration the possible ignorance of the visitors to this Museum. He labels his object stating on the label what interests him but does not necessarily explain to the public what the object essentially is.

Now I was myself a Museum official at one time. I was at the Ashmolean Museum, and one of the prides of that Museum is the great collection of Greek vases, Athenian painted of the sixth, fifth and fourth centuries B.C. with their classical figures painted, the earlier ones in black on a red ground, and in later ones, the more numerous, red on a black ground; and they were all provided with labels saying what the subject of the painting was, and sometimes saying who the painter was, and so on; but it was assumed that you knew something about Greek vases. Well, I was sitting one day in front of an open case labelling some things, making notes and so on, when there came in a number of people. It happened that at the moment—it was in the long vacation —there was being held a Congress of Secondary School Masters and a number of them had come, very properly, to look at the Ashmolean Museum. This group came into the room and wandered round, perhaps rather aimlessly; and then one man, seeing me sitting by an open case, came and looked over my shoulder to see what I was doing, and wanting to make conversation, said, 'This is a most remarkable collection'.

I said, 'Yes, it certainly is; after the British Museum it is probably the best in England'.

He said, 'It's a wonderful collection, all these vases'.

I said, 'Yes'.

And he added, 'And I suppose every one of them is genuine Wedgewood, isn't it?'

The poor man's blunder was really due to the lack of proper labelling, because it was never stated on a label that these were Attic vases of so many centuries before Christ. One did get that sort of experience sometimes in the Ashmolean Museum. Sometimes the thing spoke for itself.

There was a gallery upstairs of Egyptian antiquities and in the middle of it there was an enormous glass case measuring about 10 feet either way, in which were put things like painted wooden coffins from Egyptian tombs, and there were a couple of mummies I think, and so on. I had received a request from some scholar abroad to check or copy an inscription painted on the inside of one of these coffins. It was an enormous coffin, the outer case which had contained an inner coffin, and I found that the only way in which I could check the text was by getting inside the coffin; so I took down the glass side of the case and I was actually lying on my stomach checking the hand-copy of the inscription by the original in front of my eyes. (I may say that the sides of the coffin were about four feet high.) Now at that time, it was also in the long vacation, there was a Congress of Nonconformist Clergy being held in Oxford, and a body of those came into the Egyptian gallery and they came along to this big case—not the side where I had opened it but on the other side, and there on a glass shelf there were some clay vases with a label to say that they were found at Coptos, a place in Egypt.

The group of clergy stopped in front of that and one of them, an old man, read the label and said, 'Now that is really interesting because Coptos is, I believe, identified by scholars with a place anciently called Caphtor which is the same as the name of Crete; and that is important because somewhere or another—it must be somewhere in the Old Testament— there is a statement connecting Egypt and Caphtor or Crete. I cannot remember where it comes now'. I, inside the coffin, heard this; I didn't know who the people were, but I heard that remark, and quite unconsciously (I can assure you it

A voice from the tomb

was not premeditated) I heard my own voice saying 'Gen. 10, 13'. The poor parsons couldn't see me, but they heard a voice from the tomb giving them a biblical quotation. There was nearly a panic, and I had to climb out from the sarcophagus and explain that I was only there by accident and that I had only spoken by accident. I was devoutly thanked by the old gentleman for having given him just that information that he had forgotten, and as soon as I could I hurried back to my official study to look up and find out whether there was any truth in what I had said. By some extraordinary coincidence I had said it right. I didn't really know the reference, it was purely sub-conscious on my part.

Labelling can be a tricky business and may sometimes display not an excess of knowledge on the part of the labeller, but the reverse.

Many years ago T. E. Lawrence and myself were in Beirut, and we went to the American University there where they had a museum of antiquities collected in that part of the Lebanon and arranged for exhibition by the Professor of Latin in the University. We were going round, and suddenly Lawrence, looking at a desk-case, began to laugh. I looked at him, and he said 'Oh, do come and look at this !'

I went along. The desk-case was very neatly lined with red velvet, and in the middle of it was an object with a large label underneath, very carefully done, and the label said 'A bronze object with a reptilian body and a bull's head, found at' such-and-such a village in the Lebanon, 'a votive object, probably Hittite'.

Then I began to laugh too; and at that moment the curator, the Professor of Latin, came into the gallery and, seeing us laughing, asked 'What's the matter?'

So I said, 'Well, Professor, as a matter of fact we were laughing at this label'. He came and looked, and said, 'What is there to laugh at?'

I replied, 'Well, two or three things; in the first place though it looks like bronze it is not a bronze object at all. The description following that is all right, but it is not a votive object and it isn't Hittite !'

He said, 'You've got no business to say a thing like that. We don't know for certain what it is, and I shouldn't be prepared to say, but you cannot deny that a thing is Hittite unless you can definitely assert what it is'.

I answered, 'You're quite right, Professor, but I can definitely assert what it is'.

He demanded, 'What is it?'

I said, 'Well, it's English, and it's an ox-head tin-opener . . .'

About two years after that I was asked to re-arrange that museum, and full of interest I went along first of all to see the same spot, and there I saw the case with its nice red velvet, faded very much, but the mark where the object had lain and protected the velvet from the sun you could see. The tin opener was no longer there, but I found it in a drawer with its original label carefully preserved. I don't think the Professor believed for a moment what I had told him.

A tin opener

Naturally, out East one was constantly being offered antiquities, but the buying of them might be a risky thing; sometimes amusingly so.

I was standing one day with T. E. Lawrence on what was going to be the platform of what was going to be a railway station, when the Germans were building the Bagdad railway. We knew that there was a construction train coming along and we meant to cadge a ride on it, when suddenly a native came up to Lawrence and, pulling him to one side, asked if he was interested in antiquities, Lawrence said 'Yes,' so the man produced a cylindrical seal. These are small things about an inch long, cylinders, with a hole in the middle, and sometimes beautifully engraved. They were used for rolling out on a clay tablet, and the impression was equivalent to the signature of one of the parties to a contract. In date they may be anything from 3000 to 1000 B.C.

Lawrence took this cylinder and examined it, and then began to laugh. I said, 'What is the matter?' He said, 'Oh, do look at this!'

I took it. It was made of haematite, an extremely hard stone and finely polished. The first thing I saw was a figure of a lion beautifully carved in intaglio, and I turned it round to see the next figure, then I too began to smile. There was a procession of animals carved all round the stone, which is quite a usual design, and the first figure I had seen was a lion, but the second was a giraffe. Now, it was extraordinary that an African animal like a giraffe should get on to a stone carved somewhere in Turkey or Northern Syria, thousands of years ago.

I turned it again, and there was a kangaroo!

Obviously a technically skilful forger, with the proverbially dangerous little learning, knowing that a procession of animals was the right thing for a cylinder seal, had taken a natural history book and copied the illustrations! People did all sorts of funny things like that.

Lawrence and I were one day in the room of a Syrian banker, who as a sideline dealt illegally in antiquities, and I said, 'Have you got anything very good?' He said, 'Yes, marvellous!' I asked, 'What is it?'

He went to the cupboard, or to a safe rather, unlocked it and took out something. I really did gasp when I saw it. There was a hemispherical terracotta bowl with reliefs on it. It was covered with a yellow glaze; the reliefs consisted of a band of grape vine coiled round the bowl with the leaves in high relief; they were green, and there were purple clusters of grapes hanging down. The inside was plain yellow. I had seen the same sort of design on Roman things, and I had seen one or two pieces of Roman glaze remotely like this but not nearly so elaborate; it was by far the finest piece of its kind one could imagine. I just got a glimpse of it.

Lawrence took it first, and as we were in the rather gloomy sitting room, took it over to the window to examine it while I stopped where I was, talking to the banker. Then Lawrence came back and handed the bowl to me. I said, 'What's it like?' Lawrence said, 'Taste it'. I began to see what he meant.

I walked to the window and, turning my back on the banker, put the thing to my lips and tasted it. And sure enough I could taste the spirit gum which had fixed the loose fragments of iridescent film from glass bottles over the modern oil paint.

The bowl itself was a genuine Roman bowl of plain red ware, and someone had painted it in oils, and then covered it with flakes of iridescent glass which looked as if a real glaze had decayed, half hiding the design. The whole thing was a complete forgery from beginning to end, except that it was a Roman pot made to look unlike what it ever looked like in Roman antiquity. That was a common trick.

A dealer once told me he had got a lovely thing. I enquired what it was. He said, 'I've got a Byzantine tile more than a foot square, glazed in colour and with figures on it, and there's nothing like it in the world'.

I said, 'All right, I'd like to see it'.

'Well, come along and see it, but I warn you it will cost you a thousand pounds.'

I said, 'That sounds to me excessive, but I'd like to see it'.

So I went along, and I saw a large tile with a ridge underneath on one side, which was the shape of an ordinary big Roman tile, but the top of it was entirely covered with decayed glaze in which I could see patches of colour, but that was all.

The dealer took a piece of rag and dipped it in water, and passed it over the tile, and then I could see a complete picture in colour. I thought it looked very funny, so I tasted the thing, and I tasted the spirit gum again. Then I looked more carefully and said, 'Will you give me a pocket knife?' and he did. I put the blade to the corner of the tile and lifted up the paper on which was printed a German coloured woodcut of Abraham's sacrifice of Isaac, which had simply been glued on to a Roman tile and covered with a film of iridescent glass.

I said to him, 'I'm very sorry, but this is a complete forgery'. He said, 'It's nothing of the kind'.

I said, 'It is a forgery—it is a palpable forgery, you can see it for yourself—here is the paper'.

He said, 'I paid £100 for it myself, so I know it's genuine'.

Actually, at one time I was completely taken in. I was really shocked. In Crete in the early years of this century I was stopping with Arthur Evans when he was excavating at Knossos, and one day he got a message from the police at Candia asking him to come to the police station, so we went together—he, Duncan Mackenzie who was his assistant, and myself. And the most surprising thing had happened.

Evans for years had employed two Greeks to restore the antiquities which he had found. They were extraordinarily clever men—an old man and a young one—and he had trained them, and they had worked under the artist whom he employed there, and they had done wonderful restorations for him. Then the old man got ill and at last the doctor told him he was going to die.

He said, 'Are you sure?' The doctor said, 'Yes, I'm afraid there's no hope for you at all'.

'Right', he said. 'Send for the police.' The doctor said, 'You mean the priest'. 'No I don't', he said. 'I mean the police.' He insisted, and they sent for the police, and the police came and asked him, 'What on earth do you want?'

'Now I can tell you', said the sick man. 'I'm going to die, so I'm all right, but for years I've been in partnership with George Antoniou, the young fellow who works with me for Evans, and we have been forging antiquities'.

'Well', said the policeman, 'I don't know that that concerns me.' 'Yes,' he said, 'it does. Because we've sold a statuette of gold and ivory which was supposed to be a Cretan one to the Candia Government Museum, and that's a criminal offence. George is a scoundrel and I hate the fellow, and I've been waiting for this moment to give him away. Go straight to his house and you'll find all the forgeries and all our manufacturing plant there.'

The police went, they raided, and they found exactly what he said, and they asked Evans to come and look, and I never saw so magnificent a collection of forgeries as those fellows had put together.

There were things in every stage of manufacture. For instance, people had been recently astounded at getting

A magnificent collection of forgeries

what they call chryselephantine statuettes from Crete; statuettes of ivory decked out with gold—there is one in the Boston Museum and one at Cambridge, and one in the Cretan Museum at Candia. These men were determined to do that sort of thing, and they had got there everything, from the plain ivory tusk and then the figure rudely carved out, then beautifully finished, then picked out with gold. And then the whole thing was put into acid, which ate away the soft parts of the ivory giving it the effect of having been buried for centuries. And I didn't see that anyone could tell the difference!

Then they had got Greek coins. Those are sometimes very rare and of immense value; recently one Greek coin at a London sale fetched £3,100; another fetched £2,300—both unique coins. Of course, such coins are generally the treasured possessions of different museums. The two Greeks wrote round to the museums where there were unique coins and asked to be supplied with plaster casts of them. That is a very common request and it is always granted.

They got the plaster casts, and they had discovered how to make a steel mould from the plaster, so they cast steel moulds from the two sides of the coin, making one as an anvil and the other as a hammer-head. They looked up the catalogues of the coin collection from which the cast came, and they found there the exact weight of the coin in milligrams. It would also give the exact character of the alloy, the silver alloy of which the coin was made. So they imitated the alloy, cut off a lump of the right weight exactly, heated it almost to melting point and put it on the anvil and struck it with the hammer in the fashion of the ancient coiner, and produced something so like the original that nobody could have told the difference. They had got about 100 of these forgeries in stock, and how many of such may have found their way on to the market I don't know, but it really was bewildering.

I said to Evans, 'I shall never buy a Greek antiquity'.

He said, 'Well, even I feel rather doubtful now,' and he was a marvellous judge.

I remember a thing Evans did when he was a young man. He was touring about in Eastern Europe and went to one place, near Belgrade I think it was, where there was a private collector who had made a wonderful collection of ancient Eastern European coins, specialising in those. Evans looked at his collection and was full of admiration, and then said, 'You know, a man like you is very lucky. We in the West are constantly confronted with forgeries and imitations, whereas here I imagine there is nothing of the kind. Have you ever been faced with a forgery?'

At first he said, 'No, never,' then he corrected himself. 'Yes, I beg your pardon, once, and that was my own fault'.

Evans asked, 'What do you mean?'

'You see this silver coin here,' said the collector. 'I bought it from a peasant and it was absolutely unique, an unknown coin, and I paid the man very handsomely for it because I wanted to encourage people to bring me coins. Well, sometime afterwards another man brought me another of the same sort, not quite identical; then another came, and it went on until I discovered that really they had found a complete hoard of similar coins all together and were selling them one by one to keep the price up. A good many had gone abroad, and I told them that I had got enough and didn't want any more. Then one day a young fellow turned up and produced one of these coins with an air of importance, and I told him that I had got all I wanted of this sort, and then foolishly said, "Of course, if it had been a gold coin I should have bought it, but no gold coin of that type is known".

'He went off. A month or two later a young fellow turned up—not the same man—and produced a gold coin of that type, and I bought it. Then, after the fellow had gone, I examined it very carefully and found it was a forgery.'

Evans asked, 'How could you tell?'

'Well,' he said, 'look here. Take a very powerful glass and see—it has been cast, of course, but it has been finished by hand. Under the powerful glass you can see that the handwork was done with a tool with a minutely serrated edge. Now that's a tool that our modern goldsmiths use, but it was never known in antiquity, so I knew the thing was a forgery. I enquired, and found out the name of the man who had brought it to me, and he himself was a jeweller and his name was Alexander Larides. That is the only time I have ever been taken in.'

Evans examined the tiny tool-marks, and was convinced in due course. He went on his travels, and one day he was in a church a long way from Belgrade, looking at an ancient icon, or reliquary, which was very interesting archaeologically. A man came in and said, 'There is someone outside who wants to see you'. So Evans went out, and there was a young man sitting on horseback who said, 'Are you the Englishman going about who is interested in antiquities?' Evans said, 'Yes'.

'Well,' he said, 'what do you think of this?' and from his pocket he pulled a golden crucifix.

It was obviously Byzantine, very beautifully done, with a Greek inscription at the back of the cross. Evans looked first at the figure and, he told me, was very much impressed. Then he turned it over and looked at the Greek inscription. He saw there were Greek letters but no words that made sense; it wasn't a proper inscription at all. Then an idea struck him, and he took out his own powerful reading glass, which he always carried, and with it he could distinctly see the marks of the serrated tool that the coin collector told him about. When he began to examine it so minutely, the fellow on horseback got a little nervous and said, 'Well, what do you think of it?'

'Oh,' said Evans, 'it's magnificent, it's glorious, and most important.'

'Important?' said the man. 'Oh yes, most important, especially that inscription.' The fellow said, 'The inscription?'

'Yes,' said Evans. 'Of course, the actual crucifix is a very beautiful thing, but what gives it its value is the inscription on the back.' The man asked 'Why?'

Evans said, 'Well, haven't you read it?' 'Oh no,' said the man, 'I don't know any Greek.' Evans said, 'Well, shall I read it to you?' The man said, 'Do'.

So Evans held this thing in his hand and said, 'I, the Holy Cross which cannot lie, was made in the year 1881 by the scoundrelly goldsmith Alexander Larides'.

The young man gave a yell and snatched it out of his hand, and galloped off.

Rascality where antiquities were concerned was not always confined to the dealers.

I was in Naples, staying with a friend of mine, an Englishman who had lived all his life in Naples, and one day there came along a plumber who had a little house and a small business at a place called Pozzuoli, which is on the outskirts of Naples to the north, and he said he had heard I was there and that he had something of interest to report. He had been enlarging his house, and in digging the foundations he had come upon a number of blocks of marble, some of which were covered with inscriptions and one was carved. He had shown this to his local priest who thought the things were interesting and important, and he wanted to know whether I would come and look, and buy anything that I wanted.

I went along, and there was, among a number of inscriptions, a very large marble slab, about 6 feet high or rather more, and about 5 feet across, with a group of life-size figures carved, one in high relief and two in lower relief. The one in high relief was obviously a member of the Imperial Family of the Emperor Augustus, and the other two were soldiers, and I realised that it was a fragment of an extraordinarily important and beautiful monument.

I said to the man, 'This is absolutely first-class! It's worth a great deal of money, but I can't buy it.' He said, 'Why not?' So I explained. 'In the first place, I could never get it out of the country, and in the second place I haven't got the money to pay for a thing of that sort.'

He said, 'Well, what am I to do?' and I told him, 'There is only one thing you can do. Nobody can smuggle a thing of that size out of Italy, and if you try you will get into frightfully serious trouble. Go to the Naples National Museum and report what you have found. They will send a proper man along, and they will then take the things and value them, and pay you three-quarters of the sum. They keep one-quarter for the Government, but you will get quite a large sum of money, and that is the best thing you can do'.

He didn't like it—he didn't want to get the Government

in at all; but in the end he thought perhaps he had better do what I had told him, and he went and reported it. And the second man in the Museum, who was an Inspector of Antiquities, came to the house. He saw these things and said, 'What a lot of fuss you are making about nothing. Those inscriptions are of interest to us, but they have no commercial value, so I'll take them away and there is no payment for them'.

The plumber asked, 'What about this carving?'

'That!' he said, 'Good heavens! It's absolute rubbish, not worth anything at all—you would be very lucky if anybody gave you £5 for a thing like that. I don't want it, I will leave it in your hands. The Museum is not interested in a thing of that sort!' And he went off with the inscriptions.

The plumber came to me a few days later and told me the story. 'It is very disappointing,' he complained, 'I thought I was going to get quite a large sum of money, and I am getting nothing at all.'

'Well,' I said, 'I can't understand it. That is a very valuable object.'

He said, 'Well, I don't know about that, but yesterday a man did come along' (and he gave me a description of the man and his name). 'He offered me £10 for it—shall I take it?'

I said 'No', and made certain enquiries. The man was an antiquity dealer, and was the brother-in-law of the Inspector, and the whole thing was a put-up job. So I saw the plumber again and explained to him what the law was. I said:

'If they don't want it, they ought to give you a permit for export. I have told you I can't afford to pay the value of the object, and you have got to remember that if you sell it abroad a third of the sum goes to the Government in tax. I can only afford to pay you £60, but you can tell them it has been sold for £100, and I will pay them the £33. That is all the money I can lay my hands on, and it is nothing like the value of the object, but if you would like to sell it to me on those terms and if you get the permit to export, I'll take it.'

He said that was very nice of me, and he would be delighted to do it. So he went round to the Museum, saw the Inspector of Antiquities and said, 'About this stone you don't want, will you give me permission to export?'

The Inspector said, 'You ignorant peasants! You are such fools! You think because a man comes along and offers you a pound or two more than another, and says he wants to export it you are going to profit; but actually you're not, because you have to pay a third to the Government. Now I suppose someone has offered you £15—well, the most you'll get is £10.'

'Oh no,' said the plumber, 'I am going to pay you £33.'

The Inspector said, 'What?'

He repeated, 'I am going to pay you £33, a third of the price of the thing.'

The Inspector said, 'Look here, you are not going to have authority to export at all. The Museum is not going to take over your sculpture; it's going to remain in your hands, and it is valued at £4,000. I shall put it on the list of National Monuments. You are going to be responsible to the Government for the safeguarding of a £4,000 object. It is at your risk if anything happens to it.'

The poor man came round to me in tears. He said, 'You have ruined me', and he told me the whole story.

This was in front of my friend, who listened carefully and then said, 'Well, I think, you know, we have got to take a strong line'.

I said, 'Right, I would do anything. The Inspector is an absolute scoundrel, I would do anything to down him.'

He said, 'That's all right if you will give me a free hand —will you?' To which I agreed.

Now at that moment in Italy, the Government party had in Parliament a majority of one. Suddenly the Prime Minister received a letter sent from Naples and signed by a well-known citizen of Naples, saying that it was requested that the Government would appoint a Royal Commission to remove a certain Roman sculpture from the list of National Monuments on which it had been placed by the local

Inspector of Antiquities, which made it a thing immovable. The Commission were to remove it from the list and give authority to the peasant owner to export it; failing which, as the result of the sudden and unexpected demise of the three sitting members of Parliament for Naples (who all supported the Government), opposition members would be elected and the Government would fall. The fact was that we had got that secret society called the Camorra to back us, and the Camorra could do anything.

Within three days a Royal Commission came down and hurriedly altered the list of the National Monuments of the South of Italy, and gave permission to export the Pozzuoli stone. And it went off, and is now in Philadelphia—(I was working for Philadelphia at the time). Nobody looking at it in the Museum now would ever imagine that there had been that drama behind the scenes. Actually the Italians themselves did not know what had happened.

About a month later I went into the office of the Inspector of Antiquities, and on the table was a copy of the most recent issue of the Government publication reporting discoveries of antiquities in the country, and there was a large photograph of this particular Augustan monument. When the Inspector came into the room—he was out when I first went in—I said, 'Oh, Doctor Gabrici, what a lovely thing this is! I'll go and have a look at it—is it down in the Gallery yet?'

He said 'No'.

'Is it in one of your stores still?' He said 'No'.

'Where is it?' He said 'It has been exported'.

I exclaimed, 'Why, Doctor Gabrici, you couldn't allow a thing like that to go—it's a National Monument! It's a treasure! Whatever induced you to allow anyone to take it out of the country?'

And he looked at me, and I looked at him, and he didn't know what to say. He didn't know whether I was responsible, and I wasn't going to tell him; but he never gave an explanation of why it had gone, which was his own fault entirely.

Another curious experience occurred to the late Lord Caernarvon, the man who discovered the famous Tomb of Tutankhamen. He was a very keen collector of Egyptian antiquities, and one day he was in his hotel in Cairo and a man came in and asked to see him, and then said, 'You collect antiquities?'

'Yes,' said Caernarvon.

'Well, I've got something wonderful. Wonderful!'

Caernarvon said, 'What is it, show me.'

'Oh,' he said, 'I can't show you here. It's in my house.'

'Well,' said Caernarvon, 'If it is as good as all that I'd like to see it.'

The man said, 'Yes, you can come and see it, but on my terms'.

'Oh, what are those?'

'You have got to come at night, and you have got to submit to being blindfolded and I shall take you to my house, because I don't want you to know where it is. And,' he said, 'you have got to bring with you £300 in gold.'

Now that sounded an impossible condition. To go with an unknown man, blindfolded and with three hundred gold pounds in your pocket, is not a thing that an ordinary man would do. But Lord Caernarvon was completely reckless and fearless. He said, 'Oh certainly, I will do that,' and he added, 'Is that the price you're asking?'

'Yes,' said the man, 'it's £300, and I'm not taking a penny less, but for £300 you can have the things if you like.'

So that night after dinner three men came in and said to Caernarvon, 'Come along', and they took him outside the hotel and on the pathway of the street they carefully blindfolded him and they put him into a carriage and drove for a time and then they took him out and took him inside a house and undid his eyes. He said, 'Where are the antiquities?' and they showed him two objects. One was a small vase of polished stone with a gold cover to it and on the cover was engraved a cartouche of one of the earliest known Pharaohs, a Pharaoh of the First Dynasty. It was a marvellous thing. And the other was even more remarkable. It was a beautifully made flint knife about 8 inches long, beautifully worked and it had a handle of gold embossed with animal figures. It was clearly earlier than the first Pharaohs, a pre-historic antiquity, and Caernarvon simply opened his eyes and said, 'All right, I'll buy it'. He knew that at the price the things were dirt cheap, so he paid out the £300 and they faithfully gave him the things, bandaged his eyes and took him back to his hotel.

He looked at those things when he was back and it struck him that they were familiar; and he thought they must be duplicates of something he'd seen before. So the next day he went round to the National Museum of Cairo and he went to the case where some of the earliest and greatest treasures were kept, a large desk case with red velvet lining, and various objects on it; and he saw a round spot of dark colour on the velvet: the rest had faded where the sun had hit it. There was another long spot which exactly corresponded to his flint dagger; and he realised that the things he had bought were stolen from the Museum.

So he asked to see the Director, old Professor Maspero, a Frenchman, and he said, 'Professor Maspero, I want to ask you, have you had any valuable things stolen from the Museum of late?'

And Professor Maspero said, 'Good heavens, what makes you say that?'

'Well,' he said, 'I've got a suspicion about it. Is it really true?'

And Maspero heaved a heavy sigh and said, 'Yes, it is. We have lost two great treasures.'

'Have you taken any steps to recover them?'

'No,' said Maspero, 'I daren't.'

And Caernarvon knew what that meant; it meant that the things had been stolen by the Sub-Director, who was a German, and to have accused him would have caused an International incident that they couldn't possibly afford.

Caernarvon said, 'I've got these objects. I got them from a man whom I couldn't possibly trace—he was careful about that; I paid £300 for them. Would you like to buy them back? If so, pay me the £300 and you shall have them, because they are not mine.'

And the Professor said, 'Do you really mean that?'

'Yes,' said Caernarvon, 'certainly, I'm prepared to let you have them.'

The Professor said, 'That is more than generous of you; please bring them along'.

So Caernarvon took the two objects to Maspero's office and handed them over and said, 'Now I want a cheque for £300'.

Maspero said, 'Certainly,' and he wrote a cheque, handed it across and said, 'Now of course you will give me an official receipt'.

Caernarvon said, 'Give you a receipt? Not on your life. I'm not going to give you a receipt for stolen goods.'

Maspero objected, 'Without a receipt I cannot give the cheque'.

And Caernarvon said, 'Without the money I'm not going to hand over the objects. Either you give me a cheque without a receipt or I walk away with the two things.'

Maspero said, 'I must have them back, but I must have a receipt'.

Caernarvon said, 'Well I certainly won't give it to you'.

Maspero sat for a while and thought. Then he rang his bell and one of the attendants, a sort of sweeper, came in and Maspero said to him, 'Here is a form, I want a signature to it. Go out into the Bazaar and get hold of the first man you like, give him sixpence and get him to sign his name to this.'

And so that was duly done and in twenty minutes the man came back with a signed receipt for £300 and Caernarvon took his cheque and then handed over the objects, which are still in the Cairo National Museum.

The buying of antiquities can be a very difficult thing and it is not always a safe thing. It was, of course, a very popular thing with Museum Directors. There was a Keeper of the Egyptian Department in the British Museum years ago who always maintained that he would far sooner buy an object than get it from an excavation, 'Because,' he said, 'if it comes from an excavation, the excavator gives me all sorts of information about it, information about its level and its date and its history and so on, which isn't very interesting. Whereas if I buy from a dealer I can use my own imagination and say what it really is. So, I'd far sooner buy.'

Well at one time the excavators were beginning to discover the prehistoric graves of Egypt and it caused quite a sensation. Now if you go to the British Museum today and go upstairs into the Egyptian galleries where they have got two rooms of Mummies, you will find that popular attention is concentrated on one case where there is not a mummy-case at all, but a reproduction of a grave dug in desert sand. You get the flat yellow sand and the grave dug in it, and in the grave is a wizened, brown, dried-up body of an Egyptian with all his clay pots and pans and things round him; a prehistoric burial. Now that does not come from a regular excavation. The Keeper could have got something from an excavator, but he wanted a first-class tomb with plenty of stuff in it, and he might not have got that, so he went to the principal dealer in antiquities at Luxor, Mohamed Mohassit, and told him he wanted a really good prehistoric burial; and in due course it was produced by Mohamed Mohassit and there it is in the British Museum now. It is a most attractive exhibit. I quite admit that a really pernickety expert might point out that the clay pots in the grave are not all of the same date; but after all that ancient Egyptian might have possessed a few heirlooms handed down in his family. It is demanding rather too much to say that all things in the grave should be strictly contemporary.

But there was another story—a rumour which ran round Luxor and did make its way to London—which was to the effect that Mohamed Mohassit had found it very difficult to get a prehistoric grave, but he had a very rich and childless uncle, and the uncle suddenly and mysteriously disappeared and nobody ever knew where his body was; but it was suggested that if you looked in the glass case at the British

Museum you might see the body of Mohassit's uncle. Of course that is merely a scandalous rumour.

The dealers in Egypt can be extremely clever and they have got to sum up their clients on the spur of the moment with the utmost skill. There was one man, whom I knew slightly, and one day an American came into his shop and said he'd just reached Cairo from America. He'd got a lot of money and he wanted to make a collection of things that he could give to the local Museum when he got back to

A thing of no value whatsoever

America, and what had this fellow to show him? The dealer showed him various things and he did buy one or two, and then looking round he said, 'Oh there's a statue there'. Well it was a statue in granite, but of late Roman date and very poor workmanship and a thing of really no value whatsoever as the dealer knew. The American asked, 'That statue, what do you want for it?'

'Oh,' said the dealer, '£7.'

'Oh Lord, that's no use to me. I don't want that sort of thing,' and he went away.

He went for a trip up the Nile and a month later he came back to Cairo and he walked into the same shop and the dealer recognised him. The statue, of course, was there for there was no market for things of that sort, but the American failed to recognise the statue; so he said, 'I've come again to see if you have anything worth buying. Now that statue there, what about that?'

'Ah,' said the dealer, 'of course that you ought to have. I'm not asking more than £700 for it.'

'Right,' said the man, and he bought the statue for £700 instead of £7.

Sometimes the dealer may make a mistake. I once, in Aleppo, went into a shop—it wasn't an antiquity shop, you never did in those days buy antiquities in an antiquity shop —you went to a chemist or carpet-dealer or a greengrocer and that was the man who sold the antiquities. Well this man was a chemist and I asked, 'Have you got any antiquities—anything for me to look at?'

And he said, 'Oh, I've got something wonderful'.

I said, 'Oh I don't believe it'.

But he suddenly produced from a cupboard a golden head of a bull, or rather the head and foreparts of a bull. The front feet were there, the bull was kneeling down, but the body was cut off just behind the shoulders. It was of fairly thick metal, not too thick, but a magnificent piece in pure gold.

I was quite taken aback and said, 'On the whole, yes, that is quite nice. What do you want for it?'

So he said, 'Oh, I'm only asking £30 for it'.

I knew that was dirt cheap so I said, 'Well £15 is more like it, isn't it?' And I bargained with him and at last he came down to £20. So I said, 'I'll buy it'. And then I said, 'Now look here, where did it come from?'

He answered, 'Well I don't know for certain, but it was brought to me by a peasant who said he found it at such and such a place,' which was quite a possible site.

So I said, 'Right, now the man must have found other things with it; this sort of thing isn't found by itself; what else did you get from him? because I might be interested'.

'No,' he said, 'I'm afraid there was nothing else.'

'Nothing else at all?'

'No,' he said, 'very disappointing. I asked the man the same thing, and he told me that the only other thing he had found was a fragment of a drainpipe.'

I said, 'Heavens, you don't mean that?'

'Yes,' he said, 'here it is, I've got it here, he left it behind,' and he produced a funnel-shaped thing of green metal—the funnel turned at right angles about 3 inches from its lower end.

I asked, 'Is that really all he got?'

He said, 'Yes, that's all,' and just then somebody came into the shop and wanted some pills.

While the man was absent I took the funnel and I found the piece at right angles fitted exactly into the back of the gold bull's head and there was a drinking-cup complete, a unique object. So I took it apart again and when the man came back said, 'Well I'm terribly disappointed the fellow didn't find anything worth having except this head, but I'm taking the head; but you know I never buy anything without having a backsheesh—something thrown in, of course; I must have a backsheesh'.

He said, 'But I haven't got anything else'.

'Oh hang it,' said I, 'all right I'll take the drainpipe.'

So I took the 'drainpipe' and I got it back to London. It is in the British Museum now. It was pure silver, and the silver funnel fitted into the gold bull's head makes one of the finest pieces of ancient Middle East jewellery that the British Museum has got. Of course, the man ought to have been on his guard. They don't always understand these things, you see, none of them are experts, and it is a curious thing with the oriental how anxious he is to make money, but he will try to make money in the most unexpected ways.

I had one curious experience in buying antiquities. I was walking down the street in Aleppo and a banker whom I knew called to me from the other side of the street, came across and said, 'Have you bought the bronze head?'

36

'Bought the bronze head, what are you talking about?'

'Oh,' he told me, 'There's a wonderful bronze head here in Aleppo which a man is trying to sell, and I was certain you would have got it.'

I said, 'I haven't heard anything about it'.

He told me where to go and I enquired there, but found that the owner didn't live in Aleppo, but in a town about 30 miles or more away; he had come and tried to sell the thing, but had failed and had taken it back with him. This was just after the first war, at the beginning of 1919, when we were in occupation of Aleppo and governing the place. So I got into (I'm afraid) a military jeep and I dashed off over to this other town and I found my man, who was a greengrocer by trade, and he produced for me a really remarkable thing. It wasn't a head, it was a mask of hammered copper, clearly of late Greek or early Roman date, and it was the visor of a helmet, some kind of state helmet. It was worked in the form of a man's complete face, eyes, nose, mouth and everything, beautifully done and in perfect condition.

He had got a very strong idea of its value and he wouldn't let it go under £100. I knew it was worth a great deal more than that and I knew that the British Museum would like to have it, so I said, 'All right, if necessary I'll pay you the £100', and I bought it. The only thing was to get it home. I happened to be going down to Cairo immediately afterwards, so I looked in on General Allenby who was still in Cairo and said, 'Would you, Sir, get this home to the British Museum?'

Allenby looked at it and said, 'What a lovely thing, of course I will. As a matter of fact,' he added, 'one of my A.D.C.'s is going home in a day or two, I'll tell him to take it straight round to the British Museum for you.'

So I was delighted. I had taken a photograph of it: I went back and wrote to the Museum saying that they must expect it at any moment and I enclosed the photograph, and I told them I'd paid £100 on their behalf.

But time passed and I heard no more. A couple of months passed, and I got no reply. So when I went again to Cairo, which was at least two or three months later, I saw General Allenby and asked him, 'General, how about that bronze mask, did it get to the British Museum?'

He said, 'Oh certainly. My A.D.C. took it round and delivered it in person, he told me so.'

'Oh, to whom did he deliver it?'

He said, 'I don't know who it was; he didn't know but it was an old gentleman with a white beard'.

I thought this very funny, for there was nobody in the Greco-Roman Department who had got a white beard. I said, 'Well I've not heard anything about it, I should like to ask your A.D.C.'

Allenby said, 'You can't do that, he came back here and then was demobilised immediately afterwards, and I don't know where he is'.

I was completely puzzled. Later, when I came back to England, I went to the British Museum and first of all I happened to go up into the Department and I looked and there in a glass case I saw my bronze mask. So I went to the Keeper of the Department and said, 'How on earth did you get that here, you never acknowledged it?'

And he said, 'Why should I?'

I said, 'Because I sent it to you'.

'Nonsense,' he said, 'it was presented to the Museum by a young lady.'

'Presented to the Museum by a young lady! It happens to be mine and you owe me £100 for it.'

He said, 'Nothing of the sort, it was presented by a young lady'.

Well I was naturally much perturbed and I made further enquiries. I went to the Head of another Department and I got the whole story from him. It was the most astonishing thing. He had been sitting in his office one day and a card was brought to him and he was told a young lady wanted to see him, and when she came in she produced this bronze head, saying that she wanted to sell it. He asked her where she got it from and she told him she had got it from her brother who had bought it in Egypt and brought it back

38

and wanted to sell it. He was asking a very high price for it.

The Keeper of that Department looked at it and then suddenly he remembered he had been in the Director's office when the Director had received my letter, and the Director had passed to him the photograph of this visor; and now he realised it must be the same thing. So he said to the young woman, 'You have brought it to the wrong Department, it

A young lady wanted to see him

ought to go to the Greco-Roman Department not here. You had better take it round to them and leave it with them for them to make up their minds, then come again in a week's time.' She said, 'All right', and did.

He had told her that when she came a week later she should come and see him first. She duly came and saw him and he said, 'I've been looking into the matter of that bronze head and I think, my dear young lady, that the best thing you can do is to go away and leave it here and say nothing about it'. She looked very much taken aback, but went round to the other Department and said that 'On the whole she'd give it to them'. Of course the point was that her brother had stolen it, and she knew perfectly well that he had stolen it, and she was trying to pass it off and make a good profit on the thing. So even when you think you are safest in dealing with antiquities you may be on very dangerous ground. It was the last thing I bought for the Museum.

Even picking up antiquities for one's own humble private collection may provide an occasional thrill. I remember once I had gone the day before to an auction to look at the stuff that was to be sold, and I went all through the things that were in the sale. Then I went outside where the rubbish was put and I saw a stack of pictures, there might have been twenty-five or thirty. Most of them were large, seemed like engravings after Landseer, 'The Monarch of the Glen', and all kind of things, piled up one against another. It had been raining and they were all wet and miserable; however I looked through these, I turned them over one after another and suddenly saw what I couldn't help recognising with a shock of surprise as a very fine large drawing by an Italian seventeenth-century artist.

I went to the porter man in charge and I said, 'I don't think I can come to the sale, but I want to buy that lot, so would you bid for me?'

'Certainly, Sir. What figure do you propose to give?'

I said, 'I'm not putting any limit to it, I simply want to buy that lot'.

He said, 'All right, Sir, I'll get them for you'.

Well as a matter of fact, the following day, I found I could go to the sale and I was genuinely interested, so I went, and I told the porter, 'I have come here after all'. I thought, 'Poor man, he'll be rather disappointed because he'll want his tip', so I added, 'You do the bidding for me, just as if I weren't here'.

'No, Sir,' he said, 'I'd rather you bid yourself.'

I said, 'Oh really, why?'

He said, 'You see the fact is, Sir, I've been approached by another gentleman who's asked for the same lot, and I feel rather embarrassed'.

I said, 'Oh dear !'

'Yes, he's here now, Sir, and he's come to the sale too. I think it would be a good thing if I introduced you.'

I said, 'Do', and he brought up a man who looked to me like a very respectable gardener, a senior gardener, probably in charge of something and we looked at each other.

I shook hands and said, 'I understand that we are both of us trying to buy the same lot at this auction, the lot number so and so'.

'Yes,' he said, 'I want that lot.'

I said, 'So do I. Now tell me, what figure are you prepared to pay?'

'Oh,' he said, 'I'm buying regardless of cost.'

I said, 'Good Heavens, so am I. This sounds rather difficult.'

A size that fits my chicken house

Then I thought and said, 'Very likely, we can come to a perfectly good agreement. There's only one picture in that lot that I want. Now which are the ones that you want.'

'Well,' he said, 'I want those big ones. The glass on those pictures is exactly the size that fits my chicken house and I want it for the windows of that.'

I said, 'Good, I thought so. Well now I'll show you the picture I want. Come along.'

So I took him and showed him what I wanted and he said, 'No good to me, Sir, it's too narrow'.

So I said, 'All right, I'll have that one then and you can have all the rest. We won't bid against each other. Would you like to bid or shall I?'

'Oh,' he said, 'I'll bid.'

I said, 'Right, you bid. Get what you can and then we'll arrange afterwards how much I have to pay for mine.'

There seemed to be a lot of stuff for sale and there was not much bidding and he bought the whole lot for seven shillings. So I went up to him and I said, 'Right, you've bought these now, seven bob for the lot. What am I to pay for mine, half-a-crown, my one?'

'Certainly not,' he said. I thought to myself, 'Good Heavens, I've got against a tough customer here'.

So I looked at him rather coldly, 'Oh! What figure do you put upon my picture?'

'Well, Sir,' he said, 'two shillings is the outside limit, and if you give me that I'm satisfied.'

Well you know you couldn't get a nicer man than that. I paid him the two shillings and I walked away with an original drawing by Gemigliano (?) which is a thing that any art gallery would be glad to have. That's how I got it and really it isn't that I'm so pleased at buying a good thing at a low figure; what I like to feel is that I've saved a good thing from being destroyed altogether. You see, if that man had bought the lot, he wanted the glass only and the pictures would have been thrown away and this fine thing would have perished.

II

BITS AND PIECES

I must admit that when the railways were nationalised I thought rather badly about it, because I thought that all the nice comfortable friendly atmosphere would disappear from what would be a soulless corporation, and I was quite wrong. As a matter of fact, I've had experiences of my own which show me that the decent spirit does survive perfectly well.

I was going to travel to London and my railway station is on the main line, but it is a small station so that the expresses, of course, don't stop and I was going to take the local train that should get me up to London just before twelve. I got to the platform in good time, which wasn't normal with me, but I did, and I waited and waited. The time of the train was past and I wondered what had happened; because when I came along the road I ought to have seen the express that goes through to London about ten minutes before the local train comes to the station. I hadn't seen it.

So I went up to a porter and said, 'Tell me, what time does the express go through?'

'Well, Sir,' he said, 'that's the difficulty, it hasn't gone through, it's held up. They've had an accident on the engine Sir, and they're mending it and we don't know when they'll come through.'

I said, 'Good Lord, that's very serious. That means that my train's going to be terribly late.'

'Yes, Sir.'

'Well, when do you expect the express?' He said, 'We simply don't know. It may be twenty minutes, it may be half-an-hour. They're working at it, they'll do their best, Sir.'

I said, 'Half an hour, and then my train will come in ten minutes or a quarter of an hour after that?'

'Yes, Sir.'

'Well,' I said, 'I'd just as well not go to London, I'll miss my appointment. This is really sickening.'

And then I saw the Station Master, so I went to him and explained the thing. I said, 'Look here, Station Master, I've taken my ticket; I did that as soon as I came here. I was supposed by a railway timetable to get to London just about twelve and I'm not going to do it, and I shall miss everything that I wanted to do. Now when the express comes through, don't you think that if you could stop the express and let me get on to that, it would get me up to London just about the same time as the slow train would have done, and my journey would be worthwhile. What do you think of it?'

'Well, Sir,' he said, 'that sounds to me very reasonable indeed. I'll see what I can do.'

So he went off and began telephoning down the line and he came back and said, 'It's all right, Sir, we'll stop the express for you'.

I said, 'Thank you very much'.

But he disappeared and a few minutes later he came back and said, 'Excuse me, Sir. I wonder whether you would object to a slight change in your plans.'

I said, 'Station Master, I can't answer that until I know what the change is, but you know I'm always most liberal in my views, most anxious to meet people halfway, thoroughly reasonable. What is it you want me to do?'

'Well,' he said, 'the point is this. You want to get to London by a set time and we can do it if we stop the express to get you there, but you're the only person who wants to travel. Now at the next station, which again is where the express doesn't stop, there are six people who were going to take the same train as yourself up to town. It seems rather hard, Sir, to stop the train here for you and leave six people stranded at Tisbury. Would you mind changing your plans to the extent that you take the train from Tisbury?'

I said, 'I shouldn't object at all, Station Master, but how on earth am I to get to Tisbury, which is six miles away?'

'Oh,' he said, 'that's all right, Sir, that's all right,' and he hurried off and about two minutes afterwards a taxi drove up, the Station Master put me into the taxi and said to the driver, 'Go to Tisbury, go as fast as ever you can and remember you're not to charge the gentleman anything. This is up to British Railways.'

Six people waiting

So I got in, and we drove off as hard as ever we could go through the country lanes, and when we came to Tisbury, going up the ascent leading up to the station, I saw the Tisbury Station Master standing outside in the roadway with his eyes fixed on his wristwatch. He saw me as I jumped out of my taxi.

'Are you the gentleman from Semley?'

I said, 'Yes'.

He said, 'Thank God you've come'.

I said, 'Well, Station Master, it's very nice to be greeted in this sort of way. I'm glad you're pleased to see me, but why this special gratitude?'

'Well, Sir,' he said, 'the fact is that the express is signalled, it'll be here any moment now and of course we're stopping the train, but we didn't want to hold it up longer than we need and so I'm very glad to see that you've arrived before the train does.' And at that moment the train came in and seven happy people got into the express, probably much to the surprise of everybody else in the train, and we all got to London exactly at the time the normal slow train would have brought us there.

Well, you know, it was very pleasant. One felt there was a homely human spirit about it; and it wasn't a unique occasion either.

Once I had a friend of mine from the British Museum who came to spend a night with me and the following day he had to do some official business for the British Museum, first in Shaftesbury and then in Sherborne. So in the morning I drove him up to Shaftesbury where he had to consult a lawyer about a matter and I was to bring him back for the Sherborne train. And the lawyer was terribly wordy and long-winded; the time passed and I got more and more nervous: I urged my friend to come away, and at last I dragged him off, saying, 'There's only just time to catch the train now'.

So we drove off to the station which was two and a half miles, and going down a long steep winding hill, which was marked as dangerous, we had a lorry just in front of us which held us up badly, so that when we got near the station I saw the train already standing in the station. As we dashed in, I jumped out of the car and started to run over the bridge. As I got to the bottom step the train began to move. I ran up and across and down the other side and as I got near the foot of the stairs the last coach was sliding past with the Guard leaning out of the window, so I leaned over the balustrade of the staircase and said, 'Good morning, Guard, bring the train back would you please'. The Guard disappeared into his cubby hole and there was a grinding of the wheels and a lot of whistling and that sort of thing and the train slowly backed into the platform.

My London friend, who knowing that he had missed the train had followed me slowly and sedately, had himself seized by the arm by the Guard, was shoved into a First

46

Class carriage and was so bewildered he simply didn't know what was happening, but he went off and did his business rightly and I walked back, and as I came down on the up platform, I saw the Station Master, who came up to me, and I thought rather severely, said, 'Was it you who called the train back just now?'

I said, 'Yes, Station Master, I'm afraid it was. You see my friend was here and had to do some official business and it was very important that he should catch it and I did ask the Guard to bring the train back.'

'Well,' he said, 'Sir, I'm very sorry, I apologise. I never saw you and your friend come into the station at all. Of course, if I had, the train, Sir, would never have started.'

Now that's the right spirit; the fact is that people are so nice. In spite of their stations and in spite of routine and all that kind of thing, the West Country people are extremely pleasant. Quite recently I was going to London and the train was absolutely full. I tried to make myself comfortable in the corridor, when the door of the nearest compartment opened and a young man, aged about twenty-five years, got out and insisted on my taking his seat. It was charming of him, but I had never felt so old in my life; I took the seat but I didn't feel grateful a bit. Still, one *is* old, and memories go back a long time.

On one occasion I was dining as a guest at the high table at Magdalen College, Oxford. It was in the long vacation. There were only a few people at the high table and after dinner when we went into the Common Room for wine and dessert I found myself sitting next to an old gentleman, a spry old man with a nice pink complexion and a short white beard, very neat. I didn't know who he was, but as I had to sit next to him I thought I had better start a conversation somehow and I looked round and said, 'Isn't this a delightful room?'

He answered, 'Yes, it is a charming room. It's so nice to be back in it.'

I said, 'Oh you've been here before, have you?'

'Oh dear me yes, I'm a fellow of the College.'

47

So I pulled myself together and said, 'I beg your pardon, Sir, you see I'm only a guest and I didn't know you were a fellow.'

'Oh no,' he said. 'But then you wouldn't, naturally; I'm now only an honorary fellow. I've given up my active work, I don't live in Oxford any more and I'm here tonight as a guest just as you are, though by right I am the senior fellow of Magdalen College.'

I said, 'Are you really?'

'Yes,' he said, 'a very senior fellow. I am, academically speaking, a senior contemporary of Dr Louth.'

I looked at him in astonishment. Dr Louth had been President of Magdalen. I said to him, 'Sir, I happen to know that Dr Louth was born in the year 1750'.

'Yes,' he said, 'he was my junior contemporary there.'

I was flabbergasted, thinking what a liar the old man must be. I couldn't say it aloud though. But he saw what was in my mind and smiled very nicely and said, 'What I've told you is strictly true, because I introduced it by saying "Academically speaking". Dr Louth, as you say, was born in 1750, and he died, as President of this College, in 1850.

'Now I was elected a fellow of the College in 1848, and it is a rule at Magdalen that if the President comes into Senior Common Room he ranks as the junior person present; so for two years I was, when we were both in this room, the senior contemporary of Dr Louth. Now let me remind you that things which are equal to the same thing are equal to one another. You and I are both of us dining here tonight as guests, and therefore we are, as such, contemporaries; I am a contemporary of Dr Louth, and therefore you are a contemporary of a man born in 1750.'

I was privileged to dine at New College high table one evening in Oxford, and I found myself sitting between my host, Hastings Rashdall, afterwards Dean of Durham, and Canon Spooner, who was the Warden of the College. It was a long time ago—it was at the time of the introduction before Parliament of the first Balfour Education Act, and there was a great deal of discussion in the papers and in the country generally about the controversy concerning religious education in schools, and violent opposition to the Bill as brought forward by the Government. The Opposition had been voiced particularly by a prominent person, Dr Clifford, the nonconformist minister, and that evening at high table the conversation quite naturally got on to the subject of the Education Bill and the name of Dr Clifford was mentioned by somebody, whereupon the College Chaplain, who was sitting opposite to me, said, 'Oh, never mind what Dr Clifford said; Dr Clifford is simply a conceited ass'.

My host, who was a strong Liberal, at once took up the cudgels and spoke in defence of Dr Clifford; but unfortunately he adopted the tone of a lecturer instead of a person sitting at a dinner table, and he said, 'Pardon me, Dr Clifford is not conceited. Dr Clifford is a fanatic, and fanaticism and conceit, though superficially resembling one another and often confounded, are essentially different and should be by no means confused.'

Of course there was the silence of complete boredom all around the table, and Warden Spooner leaning across me with a beaming smile, said in his gentle voice, 'Why, Dr Rashdall, do you really mean to tell us that you do not consider yourself a fanatic?'

That was, as a matter of fact, characteristic of Warden Spooner; he was credited with 'spoonerisms', for which he is famous, and he very seldom made one, but that sort of remark was typical.

I remember one afternoon he was sitting in his study when two people were shown in, a middle-aged man and a tall youth. The middle-aged man announced that he was Herbert Gladstone and said, 'I have brought here my nephew, who has just gained a scholarship at your college, to introduce him to you, Mr Warden'. Now Herbert Gladstone was a very shy man, and as is often the case with a shy man he sometimes became in speech very pompous, and he went on to say, 'My nephew, while at Eton, has shown such promise that we, his relatives, venture to hope that with due application and with the same encouragement which under your charge, Mr Warden, he will undoubtedly receive, he may one day even emulate the greatness of his grandfather'.

The Warden smiled at him in agreement and said, 'Oh yes, we often find, don't we? that genius skips a generation!'

To sit and talk and tell stories is a most embarrassing thing, because one is so likely to get the reputation of being a mere raconteur and perhaps repeating oneself and telling the same story over and over again; and that is a most unpleasant thought. But it does happen to people.

I remember a very dear old friend of mine, an old man when I was young, who was a great scholar, a keen antiquarian, a Member of Parliament and an author, he was really a famous man—and an astonishingly good teller of stories, but he had the weakness of telling the same story time and time again. I can remember very well one Sunday lunch (he always used to have a large party for Sunday lunch, and he always told stories over the lunch table) when

The parrot from its perch

there were a number of us there and he started to tell us a story which I knew was a good one because I had heard it at least twice before, and looking round the table I saw that every other guest had heard it before, and members of the family, of course, had heard it ten or fifteen times and they were looking bored to tears; but the old gentleman went on and he told the story, which was quite a good one, and he came to the end of it and there was a dead silence. And then, from the corner of the room, the parrot from its perch called out 'Ha! Ha! now laugh!' It really was very embarrassing.

As far as I can remember the story on that occasion was that my friend had been in Westmorland and had been told that as an antiquary he certainly ought to go to a small country church in the neighbourhood, because there was a monument there that thoroughly deserved his attention; so he duly went to the church. It was on a Wednesday, and he got there at about 11.30 to 11.45 and he walked into the

A loaf of bread

building and to his great astonishment found that there was a service going on. The point was that in that little country parish there was an ancient benefaction by which a loaf of bread was given to each of the inhabitants of the local alms-house on condition that she attended a service on Wednesday morning, and the Rector was paid 2s 6d for delivering a sermon, and that service was going on.

In the front pew there were five old women, fast asleep;

in the back pew was the verger, fast asleep, and in the pulpit was the parson, who was a charming-looking old gentleman, white haired, clearly a keen scholar, and an enthusiast, but perhaps not quite the ideal of a parish priest, because my friend, embarrassed at finding he was breaking in on a service, stopped at the back of the church and listened for a few minutes and heard a few sentences of the sermon.

What he heard was, 'Yes, my dear friends, I know what is in your minds. I know precisely what you are thinking at the present moment. You think—oh yes you do—that the Ahasuerus of whom we read in the first lesson this morning was Xerxes 1st. But you are wrong! You are wrong, it was Xerxes 3rd!'

Present at the table there was a very famous man indeed, Professor Montelius, who was a Swedish Archaeologist and laid the foundation of all our archaeological knowledge of the antiquities of Northern Europe. He spoke English perfectly. He listened to this story and then he said, 'I myself had a curious experience in a country church in Sweden. I attended a service on Sunday morning. There was a very full congregation and the clergyman got into the pulpit and he began to preach and,' he said, 'I've never in all my life heard anything so eloquent as that sermon. It was moving in the extreme. It was a marvellous sermon, and I presently found that tears of emotion were running down my face. I looked round rather ashamed of myself and I saw that everybody was in the same condition—except one man. In a pew immediately behind me and a little bit to my right there was a man sitting absolutely unmoved, and it struck me as curious, so much so, that at the end of the service I slipped out into the porch, and I waited until this man came through and I buttonholed him and said, "Excuse me, Sir, but did you hear the sermon that was delivered this morning?" and he said, "Certainly, yes". "Well," I said, "but didn't you think it was a marvellous sermon?" "A wonderful sermon," said he. "A wonderful sermon." "And most moving?" "Oh yes, most moving." "Well," I said, "Sir, how comes it then that whereas every other member of the congregation so far as I could see was in tears of emotion, you appeared entirely unmoved?" And he hesitated a moment and then murmured, "Well, you see, I don't belong to this parish!" '

III

EAST IS EAST

I shall tell you a story later to show how the innate spirit of discipline which was, and one hopes still is, a feature of the English character impressed the French. Now here is another to illustrate how that same quality affected a man of a very different Eastern race.

Many, many years ago, before the first war, my Arab foreman Hamoudi was brought over by T. E. Lawrence to England for a three months' holiday. He spent his time at Oxford, but he paid visits to me in Essex, where I was then, and to London, and so on. He loved Earls Court and the waterchute and things of that sort, and always for the rest of his life he would talk of his wonderful experiences. One day, between the wars it was, I was in his house when there were a whole lot of people there in the guest room and he was telling a wondering audience of the marvellous things in England (including the waterchute) and I said, 'Well, you saw a great deal in the three months you were there, but what was it in all England that struck you most?'

I knew what things had struck him. When he came away from Oxford and was asked what he would like to take as a parting present he'd said that he would like one of those taps such as you have in a bathroom where you can turn it on and have hot water without any fire. He was a very innocent-minded man and I wondered what he would say about the most wonderful thing in England.

And he did hesitate, and then he said the most wonderful thing was in Oxford; and he turned to the audience and said, 'In Oxford there is a big public park and there are gravel paths through the park and flat grass on either side, and at the edge of the path there are little metal hoops in the ground about that high to keep people off the grass. Now anybody could step over the hoops, but nobody does; and,' he said, 'that is England. And that's why I think it's the most wonderful thing I saw.'

Nobody walks on the grass

It showed astonishing acumen on the part of an unsophisticated savage-looking man who'd spent all his life as an armed robber and so on; but he was a remarkable man. So remarkable that he could make his impression on a stranger, and a not very friendly stranger.

I had gone out to Syria in 1920 to carry on my excavations at Carchemish and when I got there I found I couldn't do it, because the Turks and the Arabs who were fighting against the French in North Syria had defeated them and driven them out from Carchemish. My site was in enemy hands; and though the French told me they might recover it at any moment and therefore it was worth my while stopping on, there was no point in my going North and I stopped at Beirut. I lived in the Consulate General, and one morning I woke up as my morning tea was being brought and I expected to see the ordinary kavass in his uniform but to my utter astonishment I saw Hamoudi, who ought to have been in Jerablus where his village was, in enemy territory.

I said, 'Good Heavens, Hamoudi, what are you doing here?' And then he told me. It was a curious story.

The French were fighting against irregular forces of Turks and Arabs whom they called mere robbers, but who were really a serious force though acting in small bodies, gangs for the most part. One of these gangs was headed by a young man who was the son of a very old respectable Turk living in Aleppo. The French found this out, so they arrested the father and flung him into prison. He was an old man of about seventy-two and he'd always protested against his son joining these gangs, and the young man had gone against his father's will. But when he was arrested, because he was a man held in high respect by everybody the Turks were furious and so were the Arabs, and finally one morning the Turkish troops entered the village where Hamoudi lived. They seized his wife and family and him and they said to him, 'You, of course, are a traitor. You have always been devoted to the English and you've always been quite friendly to the French, so you've now got to go and see your friends the French and get this poor man out of prison. This old fellow whom they've unjustly put in jail, you've got to get him out.'

Hamoudi said, 'How can I?'

'Oh,' they said, 'you're the friend of the French, you can get anything done and you've got to do it. So you're going down to Aleppo to do that. We're going to hold your wife and family and if you don't come back within a month with that man we'll cut their throats.'

Hamoudi couldn't help it; he went to Aleppo and there he heard that I was in Beirut. So he came straight down to Beirut and told me the story. I said, 'Is it true that this old Turk did object to his son being with the brigands?'

'Yes, he did.'

And I said, 'Is the old man himself innocent?'

'Absolutely innocent and absolutely harmless, and the French have been very silly because it's only got them into bad repute. But there it is; what can I do, what can you do? I've come to you because you're the only person who can help me.'

I said, 'Hamoudi, I can't help you beyond a certain point. Now down here is General Gouraud who is High Commissioner and Commander in Chief, I'll take you round to his Headquarters and introduce you to his Chief of Staff and Chief Intelligence Officer. You've got to tell them your story: it's no use my telling them. I'm going to leave you there by yourself. You've got to tell them the story and answer any questions.'

'Oh,' he said, 'I can't do that. How can I?'

I said, 'You know perfectly well. Tell the truth and talk to them as freely as you would to me, and possibly you'll get something out of them. If you attempt any funny stories you'll get nothing at all. But go and be absolutely frank.'

So he went. I took him there and I introduced him to these two senior officers and I left him, and he told the story, and talked to them and they questioned him and he answered absolutely frankly and they were so impressed that they said, 'Look here, you've got to come in and General Gouraud has got to see you'.

So he was taken in to the French High Commissioner; and the two officers said, 'We've got the most extraordinary man here, Sir; the way he talks is something quite novel, and you ought to hear him'.

So the whole story was repeated, and some questions put again. And General Gouraud was frightfully impressed and at last he said, 'Now Hamoudi, I'm going to ask you a question and I want an answer to this because it's something that's puzzled us. We French have always felt that we were friends of Syria. We came to this country to govern it for the time being. We felt we should be welcomed as friends and have a delightful time here with the company of the Syrians, whom we regarded almost as compatriots. We came —you seem to hate us, you fight against us, you obstruct us in every way and we don't understand it, it's heartbreaking to us. I want you to tell me why you Arabs do not like the French.'

Hamoudi told me the story afterwards and he said, 'My heart sank. I didn't know what to say and then I remembered you told me to speak to him as frankly as I did to you. So I looked at General Gouraud and I said, "We don't like you and I can tell you why—because your officers have got no tact and your men no morals". And General Gouraud said, "This is the first time I've ever had an Arab tell the truth to me".'

So he said to Hamoudi, 'What do you want?'

And Hamoudi said, 'I've come to try and get this man out of prison.'

And General Gouraud said, 'All right. You shall go up this afternoon to Aleppo in a military train, and I shall give you a letter to the French General commanding in the North, General Homdle. Give it to him personally.'

So Hamoudi travelled up to Aleppo. He went to French Headquarters there and he produced the letter to General Homdle and said that he had to deliver it in person, and although at first the underlings objected, in the end they had to give way, because he had a letter from the High Commissioner. He was taken into General Homdle and he gave him the letter. The General looked at it, looked at Hamoudi, rang a bell for his A.D.C., and said, 'I want a photographer'.

The A.D.C. said, 'A photographer, whatever for?'

'To take the photograph of this man.'

The A.D.C. said, 'But really, Sir, why do you want a photograph of that man?'

'Well,' said the General, 'I must have a photograph of an Arab peasant who comes to me with a letter from General Gouraud telling me that I am to do whatever he orders me to.' So he took the photograph and he said to Hamoudi, 'What do you want?'

Hamoudi said, 'All I want is that man out of prison'.

The General said, 'All right; if that is what you want you have got to have it. Now what else do you want?'

'Nothing.'

The General hesitated and smiled and said, 'I think there is something else you want for yourself, come now what is it?'

'Nothing else,' said Hamoudi; and then he paused and said, 'Yes, I have forgotten, there is something I want for myself.'

'I thought so,' said the General. 'What is it?'

'I want a safe conduct from your lines so that I can go back to my own home.'

The General gave him the safe conduct and said, 'That is the most remarkable man I've seen'.

It is very difficult to make an estimate of an Oriental, a man so unlike ourselves that you never are sure how he'll interpret the things that he sees and hears; sometimes his interpretation will be quite unexpected. When King Feisal of Iraq came over here for his second visit after the first war he had written in advance and told the Foreign Office that on his first visit he'd been taken round to all sorts of factories, commercial centres and that kind of thing, and military places, and that was all very well; but he wanted to get an idea of what English private life was like, and could that be arranged? And so the Foreign Office wrote to various people and asked if they would entertain the King for a night or a week-end and so on; and amongst others they wrote to Sir Ian Malcolm at Portalloch in Scotland and asked if he could put the King up. He said yes, he would put him up for a week-end. So the King arrived on a Saturday and for Saturday evening Ian Malcolm had invited a fair number of guests to a purely informal dinner party and in the course of dinner when the piper had stopped going round and playing his bagpipes and so on and all ceremonies were over, Ian Malcolm got up and proposed the health of His Majesty King Feisal of Iraq, which was duly drunk, and he sat down and dinner continued. But as the meal went on he could see that Feisal was getting uneasy and more and more excited as the meal went on; and when finally the signal was given for the party to break up and go into the drawing room Feisal jumped to his feet and beckoned to his two A.D.C.s (who were English-speaking, acting as interpreters) and hurried them, not into the drawing room, but into the library; and then he turned to them and said, 'Did you see what happened, it's astonishing! but did you see what happened?'

They said, 'No Sir, what?'

He said, 'Oh didn't you see the turn things took?'

'No Sir.'

'They drank my health, didn't they?'

'Certainly Sir.'

A set of rebels

'Yes, they drank my health but did they drink the health of the King of England?'

'No, they didn't.'

'No,' he said, 'no, they didn't. I always thought these Northern tribes were a set of rebels!'

And here is another case of misunderstanding. Between the wars, you may remember, Mussolini captured Eritrea and decided to start an Italian Empire in Africa and the East. England, of course, had a long sea coast on the Persian Gulf and Aden on the Red Sea, and it struck Mussolini that if he wanted to secure control of the Red Sea (which would block the entrance to the Suez Canal and stop England's trade with Australia, India and so on) he had to get a foot on the opposite coast, which was controlled by the Imam of the Yemen (with which we are constantly having a certain amount of trouble). So he proceeded to pay court to the Imam. He sent an Italian battleship under the command of an admiral who had orders to go ashore and present to the Imam an aeroplane, a number of machine guns, two rather out of date gun-boats and all sorts of other magnificent presents. This was duly done.

Somebody reported the whole thing to Aden and the authorities in Aden were much perturbed. They reported to the Foreign Office and said we must make some kind of countershow against Mussolini: proper presents must be sent to the Imam from us. But it just happened that the despatch went through ordinary channels and was opened by a very subordinate official of the Foreign Office who

A regulation rose-bowl

looked at it and said, 'I can't bother people higher up with things like this. Only another of these petty chiefs wanting a present; send him a regulation rose-bowl.' So, in due course, Mappin and Webb were ordered to supply a silver rose-bowl at a cost of about twenty-five guineas and this was sent out to Aden with orders that some official should carry it up to the Yemen and present it to the Imam.

Of course, the people in Aden were shocked beyond words. It was the most frightful *faux pas* that the Foreign Office could possibly make; but they had their orders, so a minor clerk was given the rose-bowl and told to go up and somehow or another hand it over to the Imam. Well, he went up, and in due course there was a public occasion and everyone witnessed what happened. There was this miserable silver bowl handed up to the ruler of the Yemen! And all the Yemen tribesmen rubbed their hands and said, 'That settles it! When Mussolini the Italian wants to make friends with our King he sends him admirals, he sends him machine guns and aeroplanes; obviously he regards him as a superior person who has got to be courted and won over. But the English—they treat the Imam like a dog! They are the people to be frightened of!' So the giving of a rose-bowl was fortunately more effective than all Mussolini's extravagant gifts had been, because it was supposed to show what opinion we really had of the country and its ruler.

A very nice thing occurred, not to me but to my opposite number in Mesopotamia. I was responsible for the Western Kurds and he was responsible for the Eastern Kurds, and the rumour had got around that the Eastern Kurds were going to give us a lot of trouble up to the north of Mosul, so he was told to go along and find out whether that was the case, and if they were likely to give trouble to tell them not to. So he went off, by himself of course, after sending word ahead that the Sheiks of the leading tribes were to meet him, at a certain place. And when he got there, there was a beautiful tent pitched and the Sheiks were in attendance. As a matter of fact, they were not too friendly; they had done their duty by meeting him, but they were a proud people and they weren't going to take orders from anyone if they could help it. They practically said so. They were quite polite—they gave him coffee and handed cigarettes to him, and so on, but he saw he had to go carefully. So the first thing he thought was that he had better frighten them a little bit. He began talking to them about the British

Army. But they knew that the British Army was down at Bagdad with only a small detachment at Mosul, and they were 300 miles north of Mosul and were quite certain the British Army wasn't going to come any further; so they were not impressed. Then he talked to them about the aeroplanes. Well, they had vaguely heard about aeroplanes, but they didn't know what they were, and they didn't believe that they could do anything; after all, a thing flying about over your head couldn't hurt you on the ground! So that argument failed altogether. Then he tried to talk of the British Navy. They had never seen the sea and they had never seen a ship, so that was a complete failure.

Major Noel, being a wise man and knowing the ways of the country, and finding that his talking didn't do any good, just sat silent. He sat silent for about three-quarters of an hour with all these Kurds around him, waiting for them to begin, and at last one of the Sheiks said, 'Major Noel, you English, are you tribesmen?'

'Of course—of course we are tribesmen.' 'Real tribesmen?' 'Yes,' he said. 'Of course, you know, in England we have got big cities like London, and people who go to cities, as you know, always lose their proper tribal traditions. Well, we despise them, but we tolerate them, but the real English are all tribesmen.'

'Ah yes' (they began to get interested at that). 'Are you sedentary or nomad?' 'Oh,' he said, 'nomad, all of us.' 'Don't you plough your fields?' asked one of the Sheiks.

'Well, of course we have some people who plough fields, and we don't reckon them as anything. But the real ones are just like yourselves. We move about at different seasons to get the right pastures, up into the mountains in the summer, the foothills in the spring and the plain in the winter.'

'Good!' they said. 'Good, so you move about with your beasts?' 'Yes.' 'Well,' said another of the Sheiks, 'Major, your animals—are they goats or are they camels?' 'Neither,' said Noel. 'Neither goats nor camels? Then what do you keep?' And he said 'Bees'.

They looked at him in astonishment. 'Bees?' 'Yes,' he said, 'we keep bees.' 'But you said you were nomads and shifted with the pastures.' 'Of course,' he said, 'you want the grass for your beasts, we want the flowers. We shift about from mountain to foothill and plain at different times of the year so that the bees shall have food from the flowers.'

'My God!' said one of them. 'You keep bees—but you can't drive bees! When we move we drive our cattle and our goats, but you can't drive bees!' 'Oh,' he said, 'if you took an English bee-herd and told him to drive camels he would say it couldn't be done. It's all a matter of practice—you drive camels, we drive bees!'

There was a long silence, and then the leading Sheik of all said, 'One more question. When you are moving with your flocks of bees, do you drive them from behind or do you lead them in front?' Noel said, 'We drive them from behind'.

'My God, the English are a wonderful people!' he said. 'Tell us what we have got to do.'

With Orientals you never know what they will believe or how they will misinterpret things. I was sitting once in a Kurdish tent and a man I'd got with me, one of my servants who during the first war had been on the Turkish side and had served in Sinai, began describing how he had been there with the army when their position was bombarded from the sea by warships which were out of sight. He and his companions were lying in trenches and the shells came over and fell amongst them, guided by our aeroplanes.

Another Kurd who was listening said, 'But how did they do that?'

'Oh,' he said, 'it was their aeroplanes; they somehow seemed to be able to tell the ships what to do.'

So they turned to me and asked how it was done. I said, 'It was done by a wireless; the planes were in touch by wireless with the ships which were far out to sea, and they controlled the gunfire.'

64

The Sheik said, 'Well, that was a clever thing; I never thought that could happen'.

And I said, 'No, of course, you wouldn't think of that. After all it's a very recent invention. Aeroplanes were only invented a few years ago, and the wireless is very recent too.'

And then there spoke up an Imam, one of the religious leaders. He looked at me with a smile and said, 'Not so very recent'.

I repeated, 'Yes, recent'; and I gave him the dates roughly of the invention of wireless and of the aeroplanes—'it is,' I said, 'a matter of not more than thirty years.'

'Thirty years?' he said, 'I should put it at nearer 3,000 years.'

I said, 'What on earth are you talking about?'

'Well,' he answered, 'you know history; what was the date that Solomon was King of Judah?' I told him about 900 B.C. 'Yes,' he said. 'Now Solomon, son of David, wasn't he in love with the Queen of Sheba? Didn't he regularly communicate with her?'

I said, 'Yes, so we are told by legend'.

'And he had a son by her who is the ancestor of the ruler of Ethiopia now, isn't that so?'

I said, 'According to legend, yes'.

'Well,' he said, 'where did Solomon live?'

I said, 'In Jerusalem'.

'And the Queen of Sheba?'

I said, 'We don't know exactly, but it might have been in Ethiopia or down in Southern Arabia'.

'Anyhow,' said he, 'a long way away.'

'Yes.'

'Have we any news of Solomon ever leaving Jerusalem to go down there?'

I said, 'No'.

'Well, how do you think he communicated with her if he didn't have wireless and how did he go and visit her if he didn't have aeroplanes? Solomon, son of David, used by the power of the Jinn exactly the same principles as you clever people have re-invented recently with all your wires and canvas and aluminium!'

Solomon and Queen of Sheba

They do believe that sort of thing, you see, and they will tell you all sorts of stories. Solomon, son of David, is a favourite character, and of him they have one very nice story which I always liked.

Solomon had to sit in the gateway of Jerusalem to give judgment, and he was sitting out there on a very hot and sunny day and he had his golden crown on his head and the sun was beating down on his golden crown and Solomon found it extraordinarily uncomfortable. And he looked up and saw some large birds circling in the air. So he called to them and said, 'Who are you?' (He twisted the golden ring, of course, which enabled him to speak to birds and animals) and they said, 'We are vultures'.

'Good,' said the King, 'you've got big wings, come down and hover over my head and keep the sun off my head.'

But they said, 'Who are you Solomon son of David, that we should obey you?'

Solomon cursed them, 'Because I have the sun on my head and it hurts, you shall have bare heads for all time to come, and no feathers to protect your skulls'. So vultures are bald to the present day. And then he looked up again and he saw some more birds, little birds, flying; so he called to them and said, 'Who are you?' And they said, 'Solomon, son of David, we are the little people of the Hoopoes'.

He said, 'Come and protect my head from the hot sun'.

And they answered, 'We are very small, we cannot do much; but perhaps if we all bunch together and flutter our wings we can keep the sun off', and they did so, and they made a nice little patch of shade over Solomon; and he was delighted, and before he went away he said, 'You have done me a very great service. You have been very nice and polite. I am pleased with you. You will each of you in future have a golden crown.'

The following week he came out again (he came out once in seven days) and he sat in the gate to give judgment; and as he sat there he saw a few little birds flutter above his head looking terribly sad. So he twisted his ring and said, 'Who are you?'

And they said, 'We are all that are left of the little people of the Hoopoes'.

He said, 'What do you mean?'

'Alas,' they said, 'what have we done that you should punish us like this?'

'Like what? Punish you like what?'

They said, 'You have fixed to our heads these golden crowns. We before have always been friendly to man but now everyone kills us for the sake of the gold, and we are the only ones left. Take the crowns off us.'

Solomon, son of David, said, 'I've made a mistake. You shall not wear crowns of gold in future, you shall wear crowns of golden feathers, and all men shall love you,' and the Hoopoe is a sacred bird in this country to this day, and it has a nice tuft of gold feathers on its head.

And then they tell the story of the porpoises. One day in the summer, Solomon got very tired of Jerusalem and he went down to Acre and he hired a boat and he told the boatman to row him out over the sea, so that he could enjoy the cool of the water; and as he sat in the stern of the boat he dipped his hand in the water. And all of a sudden he noticed that one of his rings—not the magic ring, but another, it was really the ring of the Kingdom—had fallen off into the sea. Solomon was terribly distressed; so he twisted the other ring and called and some fish appeared and he said, 'Who are you?'

They said, 'We are porpoises'.

'Well,' he said, 'you are just the people I want. A minute or two ago my ring slipped off my finger and is down at the bottom of the sea. Just dive down for it and find it for me and bring it back.'

They dived down, and they came up, and they said, 'We can't see anything'.

'Nonsense,' said Solomon, 'try again.' They came up again and there was still no ring. He said 'Go on diving', and they went on diving and diving and diving but found nothing.

Solomon suddenly said, 'It is time I got back, I can't spend all my time like this. Come up to the surface.' And they all came up to the surface and he said, 'I've got to go back to Jerusalem, but you have got to go on till you find my ring, and when I can I shall come down here and I shall demand the ring off you and I have got to have it'.

So he went back to Jerusalem, and he never went back to Acre again, but still today, when the porpoises see a boat come along they toss their tails in the air and dive down again because they think perhaps on board is Solomon, son of David.

Much of the mental life of the East is made up of, or built round, legends and stories vaguely connected with memories of historical figures.

I was riding one day, with a group of Kurds, over a wide plain, deeply covered with grass, right up in Northern Mesopotamia and as we came to the foothills and began to climb up, I looked round over my shoulder and saw the plain more clearly than I had done when I was in it; dotted with mounds, at intervals, fairly thickly dotted, and I knew that every one of these mounds meant the ruins of an ancient city, or town, or fortress or something of the kind. And I turned to the chief of the Kurds and said, 'There are a tremendous lot of *tells* here'—*tell* is the name by which we know these artificial hills.

'Yes,' he said, 'there are a lot.'

'And,' I said, 'that's a big one,' pointing to a very prominent one.

He said, 'Yes, and that's a very curious one because it's different from all the others, it's not made of earth at all'.

'Not made of earth, what do you mean?'

He said, 'It isn't earth, it's stones, solid stones all the way through'.

I said, 'I've never heard of anything like that, how's that come about?'

'Well,' he said, 'we know all about it, I can tell you how it came about.'

I said, 'Do'.

'Well,' he said, 'you've heard of Timor-Ling?'

I hesitated a moment, then I thought 'Timor-Ling, Timarlane, Tamerlane of course'. I said, 'I've heard of Tamarlane, what about him?'

'Well,' he said, 'Timor-Ling went out to conquer the world, and he led his armies and he came to this plain, and here because it was a wide open expanse he passed his army in review, and when the review was over, he said, "Now I want every man here to bring a stone and make a pile. There must be one stone for every man, it can be big or small. Set to work."

'So they did and sometimes half a dozen or a dozen men would club together, for their own credit, bring twelve big stones, great boulders—boulders were scattered over the plain everywhere. Other men just brought small stones individually. They heaped them up into a pile and then they marched away. And Timor-Ling went out and he conquered the earth and when he had done conquering, he led his army back and he came to this same plain, where we are now and he said, "Now I'm going to review my troops", and he passed them in review.

'When the review was over he said, "There in front of you is the heap of stones which we built when we started out on our conquests. Now I want every man to go and take a stone and throw it far out over the plain and the stones that are left shall be the monument of our dead."

'And that is the heap, the biggest hill in this part of the country, all solid stones and every stone represents a soldier of Timor-Ling. That is the mound of Timor-Ling's dead.'

I don't suppose it was historically true, but that kind of story, that kind of belief, in the Middle East persists for hundreds and thousands of years, and people still believe exactly what their forefathers did.

And once I was carried back far beyond Tamarlane's time. One day, when I was working at Carchemish, I came back in the evening across the site of the ancient town, which was all covered with grass. It was in the spring, and as usual there were some sheep being pastured there, and I saw a small boy—he was about 13 to 14 years old perhaps—sitting

A *flint knife*

on the ground and shearing a sheep. I watched him and, to my great surprise, he was using a flint knife; so I stood really perplexed. He finished shearing the sheep and let it go, then gripped hold of another one, brought it down and put his legs over it to keep it quiet, and turning on one side picked up a couple of large flints, knocked them together and chipped out for himself in a minute a perfectly good long flint knife, with which he proceeded to shear the sheep.

I said to him in the end, 'That's a very primitive tool that you are using, isn't it? It is not awfully good—do you always use that?' 'Yes', said he. 'Of course we used to use iron scissors, but they are no good compared to a flint!'

One was really back living for a moment in the Stone Age.

One of the primitive virtues that flourishes in the East is hospitality. In normal conditions the wandering stranger can be certain of a courteous welcome, food and shelter at any tent or encampment. Where almost all men are nomads and may at some time find themselves dependent on the generosity of strangers, such a virtue is bound to spring up.

One man I remember was the sheik of a quite small tribe. I was really fascinated by him. He was very hard up, and he had had a very bad time from the Turkish government; really he'd hardly got a penny to his name. I was one of a party, having six or seven men with me, and we woke him up late at night by firing bullets at his house, and when he came to the door and wanted to know what it was, we said we wanted food. That takes a long time, because they have to kill the chickens and make the bread, and all that sort of thing. And we sat there and smoked and talked and drank coffee, while every now and then one of my followers would turn impatiently and say, 'When is that food coming?', and the chief would say, 'In a moment, in a moment'.

We had a very decent but simple meal, and then bedding was produced so that we could all lie down and sleep comfortably. I said to one of my men, 'Look, we've got to start very early in the morning, and I think we ought to tell him that breakfast must be in good time'. Of course one doesn't pay for this sort of thing; it's ordinary hospitality. My man said that would be all right, but I told him, 'Remember the chief has got to wake his women up and get them to do the cooking'. 'Oh,' said my man, 'He won't have to wake the women up.' I asked why not, and he said, 'Because we've got all their bedding here and they are going to sit up shivering all night long'.

You can't help liking people so hospitable as that. I knew perfectly well that he had only got his position as chief by murdering his father and three brothers. That, you see, is all in the way of business; but they are a most attractive people.

With all their generosity in this matter of entertaining the casual visitor, there is prevalent a grasping meanness in money matters.

I knew a banker at Aleppo who was an extremely wealthy man. He'd got a magnificent office in one of the ancient *khans* or inns, with lots of clerks employed, and he dressed very smartly, wearing a red tarboosh and a black top coat and pin-stripe trousers and all that sort of thing when he was out of doors. When he was at home he put on more comfortable native costume and there he wore the red leather slippers which are the regular wear of the people in Aleppo. One day he was going through his wardrobe, and found no less than five pairs of worn-out red slippers.

Well, he wasn't going to lose money, so the following morning he took them round to the second-hand Bazaar and offered them for sale to one of the shopkeepers who dealt in second-hand shoes; but the man looked at them and said they really weren't worth having at all, they were completely worn out and they weren't worth more than 1d. a pair. The banker said, 'Nonsense, they are perfectly good shoes', and tried to bargain, but the dealer wouldn't rise. Now what did the banker do? He went back to his *khan* and he sat down on the doorstep of that magnificent office. He put the five pairs of shoes in a row in front of him, and he spent the whole of the morning trying to attract the attention of the passers by to his second-hand shoes, and he felt that the morning was well spent when he sold the last pair for about 4d.

On the doorstep of that magnificent office

They are a most extraordinary people—sometimes unpleasantly so. There was one curious case where in popular estimation (which counts for a great deal), a bad character was suitably rewarded. You've got to remember that all the people there, whatever their religion, are highly superstitious and accept ancient traditions which ante-date their nominal faith, so that lots of things are interpreted as miraculous which may be really accidental.

Now, this happened in Beirut immediately after the end of the First World War. There had been frightful distress in the country, an awful famine followed by plague; actually one-third of the inhabitants of Syria died in the course of eighteen months, and in a town such as Beirut conditions were really dreadful. When our troops came in, the bodies of people dead of starvation were lying all about the streets. Now there was a man in Beirut, the head of a great family of Christians, called the Sursoks. He was a very wealthy man who owned a lot of land, and all through the town he had got empty houses which he had transformed into granaries,

73

and they were filled with grain while the people were dying of hunger. He was waiting for the price of grain to go higher and higher, and higher. Of course everybody knew he had got the grain, but it was a law-abiding country and he was a rich and powerful man, and they could do nothing.

And then he got ill, and the illness grew worse, and at last the Doctor told him he was going to die. So, being a pious man, he sent for a priest and asked for plenary absolution, and the priest said, 'Nonsense, you are not going to get any absolution from me. Here are you, a wealthy man, with stores of grain, allowing people to die of hunger. Until you have given away your grain to feed the people of Beirut you shall get no absolution at all, and you shall die in your sins.'

M. Sursok, as a pious man, thought he had better do what he was told, so he sent for his servants and said, 'Stick up notices all over the town saying that tomorrow at ten o'clock my granaries are going to be thrown open and grain will be distributed freely to anyone who comes for it'. The notices were put up at once, and there was tremendous excitement in Beirut, and M. Sursok began to feel much better. All through that night his health seemed to improve, and in the early morning he was fitter than he had been for weeks. So he said to his servants, 'Go and tear the notices down and keep the granaries shut'.

That was about eight o'clock—at ten o'clock he died!

It was the sort of thing that in the Middle East is regarded as miraculous and, at a time like that, people were naturally much more ready to indulge in their superstition.

My house servant was a very wild character—had been in his youth—and a thing that happened to him shows how persistent the old beliefs are. Hazwaheed, that was his name, was in prison for murder. He killed five men one night and he was shut up for it, condemned to a life sentence and he was put into the prison in Aleppo. Prison in any case is never very pleasant, but for a prisoner Aleppo is, or was— I'm speaking now of fifty years ago — an extremely unpleasant place; and among curious customs was one that prisoners were never fed. The government didn't bother about food for the prisoners.

During the day they were allowed out from their cells into a big courtyard and one side of that was high iron railings separating the courtyard from the street. So the relatives of the prisoner, or pious people who wanted to do a good work, would come down the street and put food, for the prisoners, through the bars and that was how they were kept alive. They could talk to them and so on. It reminds one of the biblical phrase, 'When I was in prison and ye visited me'. That's the sort of thing I mean. They depended absolutely on the charity of their friends or of the pious Mohammedans of the place.

As time passed Hazwaheed lived in that sort of style. And he'd always been an active man, he hated prison life and one day a friend of his came with some food and pushed it through the bars and Hazwaheed said, 'I want you to do something for me'.

'Well,' the friend said, 'what's that?'

He said, 'You're an educated man, you can write can't you?'

'Oh yes,' said the man, 'I can write.'

He said, 'I want you to write a letter for me'.

'Certainly,' said his friend, 'I will, I haven't got anything with me now, but I'll come along tomorrow and bring my pen and paper and so on and I'll write a letter for you.'

The following morning he came and he said, 'To whom do you want me to write?'

'I want you to write to God.'

And the educated man said, 'Write to God? You can't do that. You can't write a letter to God.'

'Of course you can write letters to God,' said Hazwaheed, 'and that's what you've got to do. I'll tell you what to say.'

The man shrugged his shoulders and thought, 'Well Hazwaheed's mad, but still!' So he sat down with his pen and his paper, and Hazwaheed dictated a letter, which read something like this.

'Dear God,

In all my life I've never bothered you with prayers and supplications and things of that sort. I've not been the least trouble to you ever. So now, when I do ask something, I think that, in decency, you ought to grant it. I want you to get me out of this prison. I simply can't go on, I've been in here now for two years, I'm fed to the teeth and I must get out; so please reply.

Yours faithfully,

Hazwaheed.'

So the man said to Hazwaheed, 'But what am I to do with this? you can't send it to God'.

A letter to God

'Of course you can,' said Hazwaheed, 'You've got to do the proper thing. Put it in an envelope, tie a stone to it, and take it and throw it into running water. Then it gets to God all right.'

The man said, 'I'll put it into the Koecke—that's a little tiny river that runs through Aleppo. Will that do?'

'Oh yes,' said Hazwaheed, 'that's running water, that'll do.'

So the man tied the letter to a stone and threw it into the river. Two or three days passed, and then one morning the prison door opened and the governor of the prison came in, with about five soldiers behind him and called out, 'Where is Hazwaheed?'

Hazwaheed stepped forward. The governor pointed to the open door and said, 'Clear out!'

Hazwaheed walked out, a free man. Nobody ever explained from that day to this how it was that Hazwaheed walked out of prison, but he did.

And so the letter must, you see, somehow or another have got to God, even though it was only put in the Koecke and the Koecke—you wouldn't think it was a good channel. It was the filthiest sewer, dried up in summer and full of garbage in the winter. It was really a plague to the town, and it was the only river there. It was the only water supply the people had; except for the rainwater which came down from the roof and was always conducted into cisterns underneath the houses, there was no water supply. If you wanted good drinking water you had to buy it, brought in tins on donkey backs from a spring about five miles away, but it was quite expensive to do that and the town, of course, suffered a lot.

Still, that was in the old days of the Sultan of Turkey, Abdul Hamid, very different from the kind of people you'd get in official positions now. The governor of the province, the Vali, suddenly announced that Aleppo—alone amongst Greek cities hadn't got a water supply of its own and it ought to have a water supply, and he was going to see that it did. Every Vali wanted to carry out some big improvement that was going to give him a contract, and he took a rake-off; which meant that the greater part of the money from the contract and the dues from the water supply were going to pay that Vali very well indeed.

It's quite an easy thing to keep suggesting because about thirty miles above Aleppo, this little stream, the Koecke, passed within, I think, five or six miles, or something like that, of a much bigger river, a river about three times as big, which went away from Aleppo in *slower* courses, the Santoa, and the Vali said, 'It's perfectly simple, I shall have a canal dug from the Santoa to the Koecke and that will give us all the water we need'.

So the canal was dug, and on a given day the new water supply was to be opened with tremendous ceremony. Out to the north of Aleppo, where there were gardens all along the river bank, big tents of coloured materials were put up and grandstands and the Vali marched out; all the consular body was invited, all the town officials were ordered to be there; the public assembled in great numbers, all the religious heads, the Mufti and so on, and the town band. They took up their positions there, the band played, and the Mufti prayed for the blessing of God on this enterprise, and finally the Vali pressed the button.

That was the signal for the last sods to be removed and for the rivers to be finally joined up, and all the people waited. It was in the summer, and there wasn't much water in the Koecke then. They waited, expecting to see this healing flood come pouring down through the high banks of the little river. They waited and then gradually the water that was in the river began to disappear and finally there was nothing left but mud and refuse at the bottom of the channel, because the canal happened to slope in the wrong direction.

Of course, the Vali had never thought of that, but by the time it was all done the river Koecke was draining into the Santoa and Aleppo was left with no water at all, not even dirty water, and all they could do was to block up the canal again, which meant, of course, more labour, a new contract and extra money in the pocket of the Vali. So everything was for the best.

In the East primitive simplicity is often found combined with an elaborately ornate code of social behaviour. This was until recently particularly noticeable in the Far East.

A Chinese friend of mine recently told me that the one thing he regretted most in modern China is the decay of those good manners which were the hallmark of the ancient China, the tradition handed down through countless generations. He said, 'It is all disappearing, thanks to Communism, and very soon our Chinese traditions of the best type will be a matter of remote antiquity'.

Here is an illustration of what the Chinese manners were, which was told to me by an acquaintance of mine who, before the first War was not only living in China and working for China, but had been raised—one of the only two Englishmen who were raised—to the rank of Mandarin. He normally wore Chinese clothes when he was in the country, and he was of fairly high rank in his order.

On day he was on a journey going to a provincial town, which was a walled city, and he had to get there in good time because at sunset the gates were closed, according to the old fashion, and nobody could pass inside. It was in the afternoon; he was in sight of the town, and then he saw in front of him a river-bed, fairly deep with fairly steep sides. There was not much water in it, as it was summertime, but a little mud and water, and there was a narrow bamboo bridge which he had to cross. He was being carried in a palanquin. On the top of his palanquin was a rod which held at the top the button which is the mark of the Mandarin, showing the nature of his order and his rank in it. As he came fairly close on the opposite bank there came from the town he was going to another little procession headed by a palanquin with a rod on which was the button of a Mandarin of his own order but of a lower grade. And he could see—because the bridge was not a long one—that the man in the palanquin was a very old Chinese.

So he said to his bearers, 'Put the palanquin down so as to let the gentleman pass', which they did.

Immediately on the other side of the bridge the other palanquin was put down, and remained stationary. They waited for a time, and then he said to one of his servants, 'Go across the bridge and see the servant of the gentleman in the other palanquin, and ask him to cross. You may even say that I am in a hurry.'

So the servant started off, and at once from the other side a servant started from the other man, and the two met in the middle of the bridge and conferred, and each came back to his master. The answer was that the Chinese said, of course he couldn't cross first because the other gentleman was senior in rank to him in the order of Mandarin. So he said, 'Go again, and tell him that rank doesn't matter so much. I can see that he is far senior in years to myself, and years in China count for an enormous amount; age is everything. Therefore I ask my senior to cross in front of me.'

And again the servants went forward and met in the middle of the bridge. They came back, and more messages passed from one to the other, each side firmly refusing to take precedence. Meanwhile the sun was getting low in the heavens, and my English friend was growing rather nervous as to whether the town gates would close before he got there, so with a bright inspiration he said to his servants, 'Pick up the palanquin. The banks are not so steep as all that, and there's not too much mud at the bottom. We are going to wade through the river and out on the other side.'

They lifted him up, they carried him down, and they got up the other side, and there, when they reached the other side of the bridge, was the other palanquin and the Chinese occupant had got out and was standing ready to meet them.

When he saw him (as a matter of fact, my friend was wearing European dress at the time), the old Chinese looked at him and said, 'But this is a marvellous thing! To think that a foreigner, not even Chinese at all, should have such perfect manners as you have shown! I have lived a long life, I have had much enjoyment in my life, a great deal of happiness. Sometimes I have felt that I had lived long enough, but I thank heaven that I have been preserved until today, so that I might see such perfect manners, and that from a foreigner.'

My friend said, 'That is quite all right, you know. You

are so much older than I am that I thought I couldn't possibly cross in front of you.'

'Ah,' said the Chinese, 'manners like yours must be the result of constant practice and of many years of learning. Tell me how old are you?'

He said, 'I am 45'.

The Chinese looked at him and said, 'Heavens! I thought that I had met the supreme example of good manners, and now on top of that I have encountered such modesty as history has never yet recorded. Your manners could only be what they are if you were at least 87 years old!'

Of course, that sort of thing could be carried to excess and topple over into absurdity, as in another story told me by the same friend.

It happened that he was in Pekin when news came that in an outlying Province of the Chinese empire two European missionaries had been brutally murdered. The representatives of the countries to which the missionaries belonged were instructed by their home authorities to make a formal complaint and to demand drastic action by the authorities. So they duly applied to the Chinese Government, and the Government said, 'This is a lamentable occurrence, but the Chinese Government does its duty in these conditions: the criminals who killed your compatriots will of course be arrested at once and duly punished.' Needless to say the representatives of the Great Powers didn't believe that for a moment, so they waited for a while and then asked how things were going on about those criminals.

'Oh,' was the answer, 'they are all arrested and are going to be properly tried and they will be punished according to the finding of the court.'

The Great Powers didn't believe that either; so at last they told this Englishman, who was a Mandarin and so could travel anywhere, that he had better go to this distant town in the heart of China and find out whether anything really had happened there at all. As a Chinese official, he reported to his superiors that he was going there, and they quite agreed that he should go; so he travelled off in his litter to this far-off provincial city. He was met at the outskirts by the City Officials who gave him a warm greeting and congratulated him on having arrived just in time to see Chinese justice properly done. 'For, they said, 'the men have been tried, and they have been found guilty. There were thirty of them involved in those wicked murders and we have arrested the whole lot; they have been condemned, they are going to be punished tomorrow, and you shall see it for yourself.'

So he was entertained that night, and the following morning he was taken out by the town officials to one end of the principal street of the town. It was a very wide street with low huts and shops on each side, and along either side were crowds of interested spectators, but the middle of the street was kept clear; there was a line of soldiers on either side to keep the public back, and at regular intervals all down the street there were little groups consisting of three or four soldiers and one civilian, who would stand there motionless, and in front of his feet was a wooden block. There were thirty groups, one for each of the thirty prisoners, and the officials and my Mandarin friend took up their position and then from behind them came a procession. At the head was a sort of herald beautifully dressed in official Chinese costume, behind him came a very large, stout and important-looking man also beautifully dressed; behind him came a minor official carrying ceremoniously an enormous two-handed sword: behind him was another official with a brazier slung on chains, like a censer, which he swung backwards and forwards as he carried it; then a few more people behind. This solemn procession came along to where the first prisoner was standing with his guards and there it stopped, and the very big man took the two-handed sword from his attendant and stood in front of the prisoner and he said, 'Most honourable Sir, Heaven in its inscrutable wisdom has decided that this despicable and unworthy person who scarcely ventures to address you is to cut off your exalted and glorious head. Would you kindly kneel down and put your head upon the block?'

So the man knelt down and put his head upon the block, and the executioner very gently laid the sword-blade on the man's bare neck and said, 'Honoured Sir, tell me whether this contemptible blade is of the right temperature to perform the exalted operation which the authorities have deemed it worthy to carry out'.

The man shivered and said, 'It is rather cold'.

Pardon me,' he said, 'I am ignorant and incompetent, pardon me,' and turning round he took the sword and very ceremoniously and beautifully waved the blade over the burning ashes in the censer and then laid it again on the man's neck and asked, 'Is that better?'

'It is very hot', said the man.

Again he said, 'Pardon an unworthy performer of so mysterious and sacred a rite', and he waved the blade beautifully backwards and forwards in the air and then tried it a third time, and the man said, 'Yes, that's right'. 'Thank you', he said, and raised the blade up and brought it down and the man's head rolled into the roadway, and they reformed their procession and went on to the second group.

Politeness and good manners

In like manner they went all down the town street and the thirty villains (or so-called villains, for nobody knew who they really were or whether they had ever done anything, of course), anyhow, the thirty victims of the dignity

of the Chinese Government were solemnly executed with
identical ritual, politeness and the good manners which are
dear to the Chinese heart and which they couldn't give up
even when it came to executing a murderer. I thought it was
one of the most characteristic Chinese stories I have ever
heard, and I got it from an eye witness.

As is well known, the great idea underlying the intricacies
of oriental politeness was to 'save face', or maintain the
dignity of the weaker party and avoid his humiliation. Such
'face saving' has not been confined, in its less ornate forms,
to the Far East or to past generations. Two good examples
involving Western participants may be quoted.

Not many readers will remember Kitchener's 'River War',
and the reconquest of the Sudan; I remember it very well,
and I can tell you a story about it which I had from one of
the chief actors.

Immediately after the battle of Omdurman and the
capture of Khartoum news came that a French force had
invaded the Sudan from the West and was at Fashoda—it
was the famous Marchand expedition. Kitchener embarked
a force on his river gunboats and steamed southwards to
Fashoda, where the French were camped on the Nile bank.
He invited Colonel Marchand on board and explained to
him that the country was an Egyptian province and that
the French had no business in it and must withdraw.
Marchand, terribly excited, pointed to his camp and
exclaimed, 'Where the flag of France flies, the blood of
France runs red!'

'Yes, yes,' said Kitchener, 'come below and have a whisky
and soda.' Eventually he persuaded Marchand that the
matter could not be settled between them there and then;
it must be discussed at Government level, and the best thing
for Marchand to do was to come to Khartoum and get into
touch with his Government. Marchand went, but insisted
that his force should remain on the spot; so Kitchener
agreed, but landed a British force under Colonel Jackson to
symbolise the British claim, telling Jackson that he must

cultivate the best possible relations with the French and do nothing that could aggravate a very delicate position.

It was not an easy commission. The French were, of course, furious at being thus checked; they would have no intercourse with the little British force camped close by; after a few days they posted a line of piquets between the two camps and put up notices to the effect that any British soldier passing that line would be shot, and gradually the line was pushed forward and extended so as to cut our men off from the river, their only water-supply. Something had to be done to avert an explosion. Colonel Jackson told me the story. He went alone, with a flag of truce, to the French lines and asked to see the commanding officer, and after a lot of coming and going of messengers he was led to a tent where there was standing an officer who very coldly asked why he had come?

'I made him a real speech,' said Jackson. 'I said, "I come to you as a soldier, speaking for myself and all my men. This affair is going to be settled by the politicians and they're pretty certain to let you down, and we feel that it's rotten luck for you. You've done a marvellous thing in marching right across Africa, bringing your gunboats with you, but, because the object of that march isn't attained, you'll get no credit for it. You came here and you smashed the Mahdi, so that at Omdurman we English had to deal only with the remnant of his army; but because the Sudan will remain in our hands we shall have all the glory of victory and your battle, which really did the trick, will never be heard of. It's a shame, and it's not our fault; but as soldiers we should like to make what reparation we can. It isn't much; but at least the Mahdi's flag should go to those who really won it; please take it from us," ' and he unfolded a green flag, holed and blood-stained, and ceremoniously handed it over to the Frenchman. The Frenchman stared at it incredulously and then fell upon Jackson's neck. 'He was a good sort,' said Jackson, 'and we had no more trouble with him all the time we were at Fashoda.' The story impressed me very much, and I congratulated the old soldier on a really fine piece of diplomacy. 'Yes,' said Jackson, 'it worked well. But I can't tell you what a trouble I had to find the green stuff to make that flag!'

Soldiers do make excellent diplomats. There was a good example of this, I remember, in 1922 or 23, on the Dardanelles. Our forces, which had occupied Stambul, had been withdrawn to Chanakkale; meanwhile Mustapha Kemal Ataturk had started his rebellion against the Sultan and had won over the whole of Anatolia, and had despatched a large Turkish force to the Dardanelles to stop us from interfering with the rebellion. The two armies lay over against each other and at any moment hostilities were likely to break out which would involve Great Britain in a new Middle Eastern war; the powers that be were very much perturbed and the Press was eloquent as to the danger.

Then one day the Turkish general approached the British lines, preceded by a white flag, and asked to see the British general in command. He was of course politely welcomed,

Lend me your barbed wire

and he proceeded to explain that he was in a most difficult position; could the Englishman help him? The Englishman replied that he was perfectly ready to help, but what was it that he could do?

'There is,' said the Turk, 'a certain misunderstanding. You maintain that we have come here to attack you and that you are on the defensive; we, on the other hand, say that you are preparing to overrun Turkey, and that we are here simply to stop that and therefore are on the defensive. I have just learned that in four days' time Mustapha Kemal is coming here to inspect our position, and what will he find? Here are you, properly entrenched and protected by magnificent barbed-wire barricades; we, supposed to be holding a defensive line, have never been supplied with entrenching tools, so that our earthworks are of the weakest, and we haven't got a single strand of barbed wire. Mustapha Kemal will say that I've not carried out his orders, and I shall be for it. Now, General, could you lend me your barbed wire? It'll only be for a week, and of course I'll put it all back again.'

The British General beamed at him. 'Certainly, my dear fellow,' he said. 'Certainly; take as much as you please; take it all. I'm delighted to be of any service.'

So the wire aprons were removed and set up the other way round in front of the shallow Turkish trenches, and in due course the Ataturk arrived and congratulated his subordinate on his well-defended position. And no sooner had he gone than there was a fresh shift and the British entanglements were re-erected by the 'enemy' and all the risk of a clash was past and gone; peace reigned over the Dardanelles.

People sometimes express surprise that a mere archaeologist like myself was, in the First War, promptly put into the Intelligence Corps. What made the War Office do it? The explanation of my own case is really rather a long one. What had happened was that in the winter of 1913 to 1914 Lawrence and myself, who had been working at Carchemish but had stopped work for the winter, went down into Sinai because the Egypt Exploration Society wanted some archaeologists to follow in the footsteps of Moses across the desert, and that was what we were supposed to do. And we were told that we were joining an expedition already in the field.

Moses' footsteps, of course, led us outside the Egyptian frontier into the Turkish part of Sinai, and the expedition we were joining was headed by a sapper officer who, with his assistant, was making a military map of Turkish Sinai, and we were playing the part of red herrings. Well, that was all right, and at the end of it I talked to our senior officer, Stewart Newcombe, who was an extraordinarily nice fellow, and said, 'Look, when you have done your job (he had to go to Cairo and work up his report), come along to Carchemish and stop with us'.

He said he would love to see our work but couldn't possibly get permission to go there, for the army wouldn't let him go—Kitchener wouldn't allow it for a minute.

'Well,' I said, 'if you want an excuse, tell Kitchener that our camp is within a stone's throw of the bridge over the Euphrates which is being built by the German Bagdad Railway Company, and that you can pick up a whole lot of useful military information in our district.'

He told Kitchener that, and Kitchener told him he would like him to go along to Carchemish, and he duly came and we collected a certain amount of information for him. When he went off, he travelled by way of Adana in Southern Turkey and then had to cross the Taurus mountains and take the train on the other side of the mountains up to Constantinople. He wrote from Constantinople and told us he had had great luck. He had crossed the Taurus not by the ordinary pass, as most people do, but by the German construction road which they had built as a temporary expedient through the mountains above the line to be taken by their railway, and it was a wonderful place and had the most marvellous views. But unfortunately he had not been able to collect any military information about that area, and it was very important to the War Office to get it. So would we, when we had finished our work, follow in his steps and see what we could do?

I thought that would be great fun—it wasn't our job, but it would be amusing. So at the end of our work we went down to Aleppo, and Lawrence and I went round to see the Chief German Engineer, who had his office in Aleppo, and said, 'We are going home in a day or two and want, if you please, to go over your construction road across the Taurus mountains.' He asked 'Why?' I said, 'Because I understand that you get the most lovely views from there which you would never get by going through the pass'.

'Well,' he said, 'you are not going. Who put you up to this?' I said, 'A friend of mine went there the other day and he said it was lovely', and he said, 'Well, *you* are not going. You couldn't go, because the construction road has been destroyed.'

'But,' I said, 'what a pity to have your construction road destroyed before you've finished building the railway! It sounds a lamentable thing.'

He said, 'Well, it has been destroyed and you can't go. Your friend who suggested that you should take that route, he went that way, didn't he?' 'Yes'. 'Your friend who?' I said, 'Mr. Newcombe'. 'You mean Captain Newcombe of the Royal Engineers, don't you?' I said, 'Well, he might be in the Royal Engineers, yes, but he is a friend of mine and he told me to go and look at the view there'.

'Exactly', said he. 'You are not going. I am going to see that you don't go anywhere near the construction road.'

So I said, 'I assure you, Mr. So-and-So, that we are going that way,' and he said, 'I promise you you won't.'

I knew that he was going to take strenuous steps, so we went to Alexandretta and did the next part of the way by road. Then we took the train from Hamid Bay which was the construction terminus at that point, and as the train was about to start off, the compartment door opened and a fat elderly German, loaded with baskets, tumbled into the compartment, panting with exhaustion because he had only just caught the train. The baskets were full of plants of all sorts, so when he had recovered I said to him, talking German, 'Good morning. What have you been getting here?'

He explained that he was working for the Horticultural Society of Berlin and collecting all the flora of different areas in Turkey, especially round Cilicia and the mountains. He had just been on an expedition and this was what he had got. I said, 'That's a very nice job, getting all your expenses paid and travelling round the place, and all that sort of thing.'

He said, 'Oh yes, but it isn't my only job. I'm also employed by the Kaiser Friederich Museum to collect photographs of antiquities, and I've got a very fine collection. There is a great deal to be seen round here.' 'I'm sure there is,' said I. 'Yes,' he added, 'and one day I'm going to try to get down to Carchemish on the other side of the mountains where the English are digging. I don't know whether they would let me come there.' 'My dear Sir,' I assured him, 'I should be delighted. I happen to be the person who is digging there. Do come along. Wait until I return, which will be in about four months, but do come.'

He was frightfully pleased and said he would come (in fact he didn't, because this was in May 1914) and asked, 'What are you doing now?' I said we were going home, and what we wanted to do was to go over the construction road of the Bagdad Railway. 'Oh,' he said, 'but you must! It's magnificent! You'll never see such country as you see from there.' 'So I've heard say, and I should like to go, but do you know the Chief Engineer in Aleppo? He's a horrid man and he's not only forbidden me to go but said he was going to stop me.' 'Why?' I said, 'as far as I can make out, he seems to think I'm spying and he is certainly not going to let me through.'

'Oh,' said the German, 'that's a great shame. The man is a blackguard and a brute.' I quite agreed. He said, 'I wish I could help'. 'I said, 'Possibly you can. Do you know any of the engineers at the different construction camps through the mountain area?' He replied, 'I know them all very well. I'm always in and out there.' I said, 'Do give me a letter of introduction to, say, the man at the first camp at the foot of the mountains, the one in the middle, and the one at the far end. I shall do it in a two-days journey.'

He said, 'Certainly I'll give you the letters, with the greatest of pleasure'. 'Many thanks,' said I, 'but in view of what I have told you about the Chief Engineer I ask you to make out the letter not in the names Woolley and Lawrence, but we'll say, Jones and Robinson.'

He said, 'That will be fun'; and he solemnly sat down in the railway carriage and wrote three letters of introduction for Messrs Jones and Robinson to the three different engineers.

We started off from Adana and we got to the first camp where the engineer was an Italian employed by the German Company. I found him in a raging temper. He had just received notice of dismissal because the Company had been overspending grossly (chiefly because of corruption on the part of the engineers), and as they were short of funds they were cutting expenses, 'And so the first thing they do is to sack me! I'm a better engineer than anybody else on this line, but because I'm Italian and not German they are turning me out!' I encouraged him to talk that way, and he got more and more violent about the Germans until at last I said, 'Now look here! I'm going to tell you something which otherwise I shouldn't have told you. I am an archaeologist, but I happen to be doing or trying to do a job for the British War Office. I want to know exactly how this line is planned, what progress it's making, what its prospects are, and so on. Can you help me?'

He said, 'Good heavens! Can I help? I'll give you blue-prints of the whole line and I can give you details of exactly what progress has been made in every section and where the difficulties are and what they are likely to overcome and what they can't.'

Sure enough, by the morning he had supplied me with the whole of the information the War Office could have hoped for. I put the precious documents in my pocket, and we walked on up the mountain.

We hadn't gone very far when our small party—just Lawrence and myself and a couple of muleteers with our baggage—met a German N.C.O. with four Turkish soldiers, who walked straight up to us and said, 'Clear out, go back'. I asked 'What's the matter?' The N.C.O. said, 'You are not coming along here. You're going straight back to where you came from.' I said, 'I'm not doing anything of the sort.' 'You are,' said he. 'We know all about you and I have got my orders.' I enquired what he did know about me.

He said, 'We know that two British spies, Woolley and Lawrence, are coming up this way, and we are not going to let them through'. 'Ah yes, dear me,' said I, 'very interesting. Are they really coming? Now who gave you this order?' 'Engineer So-and-so, who is the head of my section.' I said, 'Engineer So-and-so? That is interesting. I have got a letter of introduction to him. Here it is, an open letter, and you can read it, but you will find you are making a mistake, because the names are not Woolley or Lawrence, or what-ever funny names you quoted, but Jones and Robinson.'

He read the letter, and he apologised and saluted, saluted and apologised again, and said, 'I suppose they are farther down the road'. I said, 'Possibly they are. How should I know?' and we walked on.

Of course we didn't call on the engineer; we passed his camp and got safely through to the other side, for we had got all the information we wanted. It is the only piece of spying that I ever did before the War. That really was why Lawrence and myself were both shoved by the War Office into the Intelligence as soon as the war began.

Having said I did get into Intelligence, I must tell one story from the Intelligence Department. At Port Said where I was stationed, a French armed trawler came into harbour about eight o'clock in the evening and when they had made fast, the Captain came straight to my office and said that he'd seen a most important thing. As he came past the end of the mile-long breakwater, he had seen signalling from the shore, and as there were German submarines in the neighbourhood this meant information was being given to the enemy. He was quite sure it was signalling. I felt a bit incredulous but said I would look into it, of course.

And then the next night an English Captain came in and told me exactly the same story. At just eight o'clock in the evening he had been passing the end of the breakwater and he saw signalling which came from the shore from fairly high up. He thought it must have been from one of the big blocks of flats on the sea front. There was no doubt about it.

Of course I had to take serious notice, so I called the Army in and posted a Signals officer with a couple of N.C.O's at the far end of the breakwater. They went out about seven o'clock and they waited. It got dusk at seven, by eight o'clock it was dark, and they said sure enough there was the signalling. A good many lights showed up in the building, window lights, but all of a sudden one began in morse—long, short, long, short, and so on—and they had taken it down. It went on for about twenty minutes or a quarter of an hour and then stopped. As they had taken it all down, I asked whether they could read it? The officer said, 'Well, of course I can't, the thing's in code. I can give you the letters, but they don't mean anything to me.' I asked whether it was good signalling. He said, 'No, it is perfectly sound morse, but it was done by someone who isn't used to signalling. It was clumsily done, but there's no question about it. And it happened about eight o'clock.'

I thought, well, here is something serious. I tried it out a second night, and the same thing happened, though the letters which he took down were entirely different from what had been taken down the first night. We couldn't make head or tail of them. So I said, 'Now we strike. Have you found out where it is?' because I had told them to watch very carefully with night glasses to see if they could identify the building, and if possible the window in the building from which the signalling was done. He said he'd got the building without any question, he'd got the floor of the building without any question because there were other lights below which had helped him, and so on, and he was practically certain of the exact window. I then found out that the window was one in a flat occupied by a Pilot in the Suez Canal Service, who was a German subject.

Of course, you couldn't get anything better than that. A pilot knew all the shipping which would be going through the Canal, and being a German he was only too likely to be in touch with the enemy. So I decided, 'Now, we'll raid that place, but we'll raid it when the signalling is going on. He's signalling every night, so it's quite easy !'

I sent my Signals officer out again to the far end of the quay. I had a small force of soldiers hidden among the bathing tents on the beach—immediately in front of the house there was a road, then the beach with the bathing cabins. I had the men hidden there. We had a telephone at the far end of the quay, and we had guards put inconspicuously along the street to see that nobody went in or out of the building; and I waited until the man on the quay telephoned to us to say that the signalling had started. So then the soldiers got up, we made a rush for the building, entered, went through up to the right floor, and knocked at the door, and it was opened by an Egyptian servant.

I said, 'Where's your master?' He said, 'He's out with his

wife'. I said, 'Oh, where?' 'He's in the flat two floors down, having dinner with a British Pilot in the Suez Canal Company's service.'

So I sent some men down to make sure of that, but meanwhile I said, 'I'm coming in to investigate'. When the servant said we couldn't we brushed him on one side and the soldiers came in with me into a room about which we weren't quite certain (the drawing room, I think it was), but there was nothing there—it was in the dark. Then we looked into another room, and finally came to the room we *were* pretty certain about, and there we found the signalling still going on.

On the floor was a powerful lamp, and between the lamp and the window was a bath of hot water, in which the nurse was bathing the baby, and as she moved backwards and forwards she blotted out from the window the light of the lamp, and the morse signals were being given to any ship that might be at sea!

Morse signals

I had to retire feeling the most consummate fool, having set in motion all the machinery of a military raid simply because the baby was being washed punctually at eight o'clock each night!

In the last war I didn't have so much military experience. I was charged with the organising and running of the Army

95

branch for the preservation of monuments and fine arts and that meant that I was in the War Office all the time and there were not many incidents that lend themselves to narration.

Occasionally, of course, things did turn up that were rather amusing; partly because though my branch was for the preservation of monuments and fine arts people chose to interpret that in an extraordinarily broad fashion. On one occasion—it was well on in the war when we were fighting in Normandy—I was rung up and found it was the South Kensington Museum of Natural History at the other end of the telephone; someone asked, 'Is that Sir Leonard Woolley?'

And I said, 'Yes, what's the matter?'

He said, 'Well, we want your help'.

I was rather surprised, but asked, 'What can I do?'

And he said, 'Is it the case, as we read in the papers, that a large Allied force has landed in the South of France and is advancing up Northwards through the middle of the country?'

I said, 'Certainly it is'.

'Well,' he said, 'as far as we can make out they are gradually getting nearer to such and such a French town and that's where we want your help.'

I said, 'Why?'

'You're in charge of monuments and fine arts, aren't you?'

'Yes.'

'Well, in that town there is a French doctor who has got an absolutely unique collection of fleas. Would you please see that the Army respects the fleas?'

I said I'd do my best. So I sent a wire out to the Monuments Officer with that particular force and told him that the Army really ought to be very careful not to upset the collection of fleas, for their own sake as well as anybody else's. As a matter of fact the collection escaped all damage, but it was an unexpected enlargement of what you would call monuments or what you could call fine arts. But that sort of thing happened rarely.

It was during the earlier war that I came in contact with a queer little Syrian French-speaking Levantine, a man of the sort I have always disliked most, the sort I have always considered the most contemptible. They haven't got any of the good qualities of the desert Arab, they have all the vices of the town, and all the vices of the West as well as of the East. Yet one of those men was, I think, the bravest man I've known, though so nervous that I had to be careful how I spoke to him, for he burst into tears if he thought I was angry. He was a terribly timid little creature.

He was really an electrical engineer who had come away from Beirut just before the war, and he came to me in Port Said and said that he would like to be employed to work as a spy in Syria. I said, 'It's a difficult job, and a dangerous one'. 'Yes,' said he, 'I suppose it's dangerous, but I should like to do it.'

Knowing how commercially-minded those Levantines all are, I said, 'I'm afraid that I could not employ a man for work of that sort and pay him the kind of salary that you would wish'. 'Oh,' he said, 'I don't want any salary. I'll pay my own expenses if you'll let me go.' I asked him what he really wanted, and at last got the truth out of him.

'I'd like to do some work so that at the end of the war I might possibly be given an English decoration.' It was a pathetic hope, but I did employ him. He was a brilliantly clever electrical engineer, and he and the engineer on a British warship between them made a wireless transmitting and receiving set with a four-mile radius. (This was in 1916, when I had been told here in England that you couldn't make a set of that sort lighter than two men could carry.) It fitted into a little one-pound biscuit tin. It was a beautiful little instrument.

We arranged that I should land him on the Syrian coast and he could go to a house in the Lebanon where there would be trellis-work with vines on it, looking out towards the sea, and he could easily put his wires across that and nobody would notice them—everyone would think they were meant for the vines. We would have ships passing at intervals to which he would send out messages. I took him out in a little sailing boat with an auxiliary motor which I had got, northwards up the Syrian coast, and he was more seasick than anybody I had ever seen, and I wondered very much whether I could ever land him. I asked him, 'Michel, do you think you can go ashore'. And he said, 'I would sooner die on land than at sea'. So we took him, two French sailors and myself, and bundled him into a little rowing boat, and in pitch darkness we rowed him to the shore where there was a flat table of rock just about flush with the water, its surface broken up with pools and so on, but you could step across them and get ashore. We landed him there, and the first thing he did was to fall into one of the pools, and though it was enemy territory and we were running a certain risk, the French sailors laughed so loudly that I thought they had given the whole show away. Luckily nobody came, and Michel struggled to dry land. But almost at once he got into trouble and was suspect because there was no evidence to show where he had been before he landed, and the police thought he must have come from abroad, so he was arrested in the Lebanon and put under guard in a little hotel in a village high up on the Lebanon mountains overlooking Beirut. Then he was shut up with two guards always with him. He was going to be tried, but they were keeping him there for the moment (I don't quite know why) and then, largely through terror, he became ill. He got dysentery. The hotel he was in was of the most primitive type, with no sanitation at all, and every now and then he had to stagger out of doors into the fields, and each time he passed an old stone barn of considerable size, with a Turkish sentry on duty at the door. Michel just nodded to him at first, and then got into conversation with him.

One day he asked, 'What are you guarding?'

And the soldier said, 'It's a horrid job; I am guarding this store of petrol'.

'Petrol, what for?'

'Oh,' he said, 'it is for these German submarines. They come into Beirut, and then we have to load up lorries full of petrol and take it down to fuel them, and it is all kept up here out of danger because if it blew up in the town it would destroy the whole of Beirut.'

And Michel said, 'I should think it must be dangerous because I can smell it from outside'.

'Smell it?' said the guard, 'of course you can! Half of the tins are leaking; the floor is running with petrol. I daren't smoke a cigarette or do anything because I should probably kill myself.'

I daren't smoke a cigarette

And Michel went back to his prison room and sat there and for a day or two thought things over; he was intensely miserable because, as he told me afterwards, he was so afraid that as he had not sent any wireless messages I should think that he had betrayed us and was working for the other side. At last he thought of something. So the next time he went out as he passed a little brake of sugar-canes, he cut one and cut the top off and walked with this as a stick as if he was very weak, which he was, and while he was out he cut a narrow slit all down the stick on one side—just a little sliver of the cane so that it made a tube open along one side and about 3 feet long. Now at that time you couldn't buy matches or anything of that sort in Syria, and everybody was using what sometimes we used in England, those flint strikers with a long cord of tinder, and that was what Michel had got. He went back to his hotel and said to his two guards, 'It's a dull time that you are having here, wouldn't you like a drink?'

And they said, 'Certainly, but we can't afford drinks.'

'That's all right, I have got some money,' said he. 'I can't drink, I am much too ill, but tell the innkeeper to bring you in three or four bottles of good red local wine.' The guards were delighted and the wine was brought in. Michel said, 'I am sorry I have to go out again,' and he went out, and passing the sentry said, 'I think it is hard luck on you! My two guards are much better off; they are sitting there drinking as much as ever they like. Why don't you join them? Nobody will know any better. When did your officer last come round?'

The soldier said, 'He came round about an hour ago'. 'Oh,' said Michel, 'he won't be back for another four hours anyhow, so you go and have a drink, my dear fellow. I am paying for it, it's up to me.'

So the guard disappeared into the Hotel, and Michel took his long tinder cord, pushed it down the tube of sugar cane, then lit one end so that it smouldered and pulled the cord back until the smouldering end was well inside the tube, and when he came back past the barn he went to the door, which he had noticed had a great big old-fashioned lock and a huge keyhole, and he pushed his cane through the keyhole, hoping to heaven that it wouldn't blow things up at once; and it didn't. He went back to the Hotel and he sat innocently with his guard and the sentry and after about threequarters of an hour there was a tremendous explosion and the whole of the German petrol store blew up. We saw it from the sea; we knew about it, but we didn't know how it had happened. But it was done at the risk of his life by the timidest and most naturally cowardly little man I've known who, at the same time, through sheer will-power, was one of the bravest fellows I have met.

Michel couldn't wireless to me, and he was horribly afraid that I should think that he had joined the other side, the enemy, and had let me down. So he decided to get out from enemy country and report in person, and the only way he could get out from Syria was by travelling up North through Turkey, Bulgaria, Austria, Germany and coming out into Switzerland. To do that in wartime was a most fantastic adventure, but he did it, and I had him in my office at Port Said, sitting in an easy chair, a little wizened-looking man, middle-aged, shaking with nervousness (I hardly dared to speak to him in fear he should burst into tears) but giving me the most minute details in his report of enemy forces, guns, etc, in one military centre after another.

He'd started with Beirut and gave me a lot of details about the forces there, and further North in Homs and Aleppo, and I said at last, 'Look here, Michel, how can you remember that? You can't possibly remember these details.'

'Of course not,' he said, 'I can't remember, but I've got them written down. I wrote them down at the time.'

I asked, 'Wasn't that a dangerous thing to do?'

He said, 'No, it was not dangerous. You see, I went to the Turkish authorities in Beirut and I said that I was a chemist and I was very much distressed at the pestilence that was raging in the country, and people were dying like flies; as a matter of fact I suggested that I should go up to Constantinople where I could get large supplies of drugs that couldn't possibly be found in the South, and I would bring those back and do my best to put the civilian and military population into a decent state of health. They welcomed that; and I said I would do it at my own expense as a contribution to the Turkish Empire, so I had to show them something; and I showed them the addresses of the chemical firms with which I had influence and from which I could get the drugs. Well, of course, the firms don't really exist, all these are codes giving me the numbers of troops and guns.' And he proceeded to show me. It was a very clever code.

I said, 'Now, Michel, that was very clever of you. Did you do that always?'

'Oh no,' he said. 'Of course I couldn't. I had to change my method. I used various schemes.' And then his eyes glittered for a moment and he went on, 'One was very, very clever, and that was doing everything in terms of music. You see I realised that musical notes could perfectly well stand for alphabetical letters or even for syllables, and I bought a lot of properly lined musical paper and I wrote out all my reports in musical notes; and it was very good. But it nearly got me into trouble.'

I asked, 'How was that?'

'Well,' he said, 'Sir, it was all right, you see; I had got permission from the Turks to go into Switzerland as a neutral country to buy agricultural implements which the Government of Southern Syria very much needed, and they gave me permission to do that, so I travelled quite easily up to the Turkish frontier, and I got to the frontier of Bulgaria and I was sitting in the train and soldiers and officials came round looking for contraband and they came into my compartment.' (I wish I could tell you the story in the language that he did, it was extraordinarily funny as he told it, but I can't.)

'They looked into my compartment and I said, "I have nothing to declare", and they opened my bag and there was nothing; then suddenly they saw on the rack above my head another dispatch case and they said, "What is that?" and I said, "Oh, that is music". They said, "Music? let us look". So I took down the bag and opened it and showed to the man all this music. And he looked at it and he said, "This isn't music". I said, "Of course it is". He said, "No, music is printed and this is written by hand! This sort of thing isn't allowed; all manuscripts are confiscated!" I protested, "But you *can't* confiscate it! Of course it's written by hand; it's my own composition. I am a great musician and I'm going now to Sofia by invitation of the Government to give a concert of my own music." "Well," he said, "that may be, but this is manuscript, and it is against the rules, so I must call my superior officer," and in a minute or two up came an officer with two or three more soldiers and they looked at it and they said, "Nonsense, this is spy work! Come along with us," and they dragged me out of the compartment. I protested, "It *is* music", and the officer said, "How do I know it's music?" And I said, "Well it *is* music", and the officer said, "Well, I don't know anything about that".

'Then one of the porters who was standing by said, "You can easily put that to the proof. The stationmaster here is a musician and he's got a piano and he can play. He could play that and tell you whether it's music or not." My heart sank, but there was nothing to do, so I said, "Yes, let him try to play it", and I was dragged along the platform and they found the stationmaster and they said, "You have a piano?", and he said, "I have", and they said, "you've got to play these tunes". The stationmaster said, "I'm not a very good player", and they said, "Never mind, you've got to play these tunes and prove whether it's music or not".

The Stationmaster plays

'I was desperate: but we went into the stationmaster's sitting-room and we sat down there. I had my hands between my knees and I thought, "Michel, your last hour has come". The stationmaster sat at the piano and he opened the first piece of music that I'd got and he looked at it, and he looked very puzzled, and then he lifted his hands and he brought them down on the keys—and it was terrible! You never heard such dreadful noises as came from that piano; and they all looked at each other and began to smile. Then the stationmaster went on to the second thing. The first thing had been the name of the town and the second thing was the number of guns there . . . and I heard a perfectly good chord come, a very pleasant little chord, and I sat up and I said to myself, "Michel, you are a musician after all"; and the stationmaster looked pleased. The next thing was the number of troops, and that came. It was difficult to play but it sounded well, and then there was another place name, and it was terrible, and the stationmaster tried and tried and at last he turned round and he said, "This is too difficult for me". I said, "Of course, this is *modern* music", and the stationmaster said, "I don't know much about modern music". I asked him, "Do you know the works of the younger Strauss?" "Strauss," he said, "I've heard of him. He is a very modern master." "Modern master! He is old fashioned, he is out of date," I said. "This is the new music, the stuff that I write. I am a great musician."

'And they all took off their hats and they bowed to me and said, "Certainly you shall go on to Sofia and you shall play before the Government Circles of Sofia and we shall be congratulated for letting you through the customs", and I got safely through, and here is all my music. And I have got a complete list of nearly all the garrisons in Turkey.'

It was quite a surprising experience. And his was a bluff which came off. Bluffs didn't always come off in that service.

One day I was in my office in Port Said and some of the Port Police came in with a young fellow in mixed dress, partly European and partly Arab, and they said they had brought him to me for investigation. I asked what was the matter. 'Well,' they said, 'He's just got off a boat, a neutral ship which was passing through the Canal. He got off and when we asked him what his business was he said he was going to Jerusalem; and we got suspicious and brought him round to you.'

I asked him what he meant by this and he said, 'That's where I want to go'.

I said, 'Why?'

He said, 'Because I'm a Mohammedan and it's one of our Holy Cities and I want to go there'.

I said, 'Who are you?'

Then he told me his story: that his father was a Lebanese Arab who had migrated into West Africa where he was in the Spanish Zone of Tangiers; he'd had a business there and was therefore a Spanish subject, and he'd grown up in the business. His father had died and now the war had come and the business had gone 'phut' and thinking of himself as a Spaniard he had gone over into Spain hoping there would be an opportunity for him there, and he'd found there was no chance—Spaniards didn't want a Syrian amongst them at all—so he had applied to the Government for a permit to go to Jerusalem; and his papers were there showing the truth of the whole story, and because he was coming by Egypt he had gone to the British Consulate General and he'd got his passport properly visa'd there with an English visa. There was nothing to be said except, of course, to tell him that he couldn't go to Jerusalem. That he didn't seem to understand.

He said, 'But I'm a Spanish subject and Spain is neutral; why should I be held up because you happen to be at war with Turkey?'

I said, 'Well, that happens to be the rule of the war; we don't let people go into the enemy territory'.

He seemed very much distressed, but was very persistent that he wanted to go. Well, I thought, it is all mere rubbish; there's nothing that I can do. But we went on talking, and an idea suddenly struck me. I don't know much Arabic but I have lived in and worked in Egypt and in South Syria and in Northern Syria where the dialects are very different, and I suddenly began to wonder what sort of Arabic they talked in Tangier—so I started to listen, not to the substance of what he was saying, but to the form in which he said it, and I recognised a few words which wouldn't have been understood by an Egyptian, but which were understood by a Syrian. So then I tried an experiment and spoke to him in the very broadest North Syrian dialect and he understood at once and answered me and relapsed into more or less the same dialect as I was speaking. I did that for a few minutes and then I turned to him and said, 'You're a liar, you don't come from Tangier at all, you come from Syria. I don't know exactly from where, but I should say in the neighbourhood of Tripoli; and that is where you were brought up.'

He smiled and said, 'Why do you talk like that? It isn't true, I've never been in Syria, and I was all my life in Tangier and these papers prove it.'

'Those papers prove nothing. They're not genuine.'

'They are genuine,' said he, 'they're issued by the Spanish Government, and they're visa'd by your British Government, what more can you ask?'

I opened the passport and looked at it again. What he had said about it was perfectly true. I said, 'No, you come from Syria'.

He said, 'I never was in Syria. Look at the passport again.'

So I looked at the passport and all of a sudden I took a paper knife from my desk and I slipped it under the photograph on the passport and tore the photograph off—which, of course, was quite an illegal thing to do—and on the back of the photograph was the rubber stamp which I'd hoped to see with the name of the photographer and the date of the photograph. The photographer's address was Beirut and the photograph had been taken four months before. So I held the photograph up, the back of it, to the man. He looked at it and fell flat on the floor in a faint. He was, of course, an enemy agent who was coming through. All his papers were forged, but it was merely that illegal action on my part which called his bluff and proved what he was. You had to be very careful.

But you could be too careful. One day I was talking to the Censored Telegrams of Port Said who was a Scotsman, terribly conscientious, one of the most conscientious men I've ever known, and I was expressing my sympathy for him for having so dull a job, simply to censor telegrams, and I said, 'There's nothing to find out, you can't detect anything'.

He said, 'Oh yes, you can'.

I asked him, 'What can you detect, and how?'

He said, 'When I was given this job I was told to examine the telegrams not only individually but in series, and to note the kind of messages that were being sent to any one country and if suddenly some new word came in which hadn't been mentioned in other telegrams and then was repeated in a second telegram or a third, then I was to suspect that that might be a code word; and if it was connected with numbers I could be pretty certain of it, and,' he said, 'that's exactly what I've done, and I've been stopping one of the most dangerous pieces of spy work that is going on in Egypt'.

I said, 'Well that's splendid, but how can you prove it?'

He smiled and said, 'Well I've been doing this work now for more than six months and then all of a sudden I noticed a telegram, in English of course, sent to Spain, which, mark you, is a neutral country, but a hot bed of spies as you well know, and there was a word in it—"Onions"—which had never occurred before; and a couple of days later there was another telegram to Spain with the word "Onions" and then a third and a fourth; and there were numbers attached to these, large numbers. Of course, they were reporting on the military position in Egypt.'

And I said, 'What did you do?'

He smiled; 'I stopped every one. They kept on bringing me these telegrams, handing across the counter; the money was paid and all that sort of thing, but not one of these telegrams has left Egypt.'

And I said, 'My good man, of course you've acted very conscientiously in this, but you know you have made a mistake'.

'What do you mean,' said he, 'I've acted according to instructions and my own understanding of what spy work is.'

I said, 'Yes, but you don't happen to know that one of the staple industries of Egypt is the export of onions to Spain at this time of year, and you've stopped the most profitable business on which this country depends'.

I don't believe I ever convinced him, but that was the truth. And sometimes, just occasionally, you had an incident in the course of your intelligence work that was pathetic, or even tragic.

There was a plan on the part of the Army to invade Turkey from the corner of the Mediterranean where Asia Minor turns round from the Syrian coast, the Gulf of Alexandretta, where forces could be landed and cut all the communications of Turkey with its Southern dependencies. For that we had to have the most detailed maps. It's a mountainous region, and we had to have maps showing how the Turks could pass through the mountains, and how we could stop them; and I was entrusted with that job. Maps existed, but not of the kind we needed; I had to get local information. And then I found that there had been a monastery up in the mountains there, a Trappist monastery where the monks were not allowed to speak, you know; they had occupied themselves in the study of botany and the collection of healing herbs in that mountain area. That meant that they knew the mountains extraordinarily well. When Turkey came into the war, as they were foreigners, Europeans, they had been driven out and had taken refuge in Alexandria, and there they were living in a little community, in exile but in silence.

I had to get a dispensation from the Pope to get two of these monks over to Port Said to report to me on the geography of the neighbourhood of Antioch, and there came two dear old men; one was aged about 78 and the other about 85; the man of 78 was senior in rank in the monastery. They came wearing their long white garments; they had long white beards; they were the most venerable couple, and they sat in my room and I tried to ask questions of them—they had a dispensation to speak. I very soon discovered that the older man had travelled more than the younger one, but as soon as I asked a question of the older man and he began to speak, the younger one who was his senior in monastic discipline would say, 'Don't listen to that poor old man. He knows nothing at all.' Then he would proceed to tell me his version, which wasn't nearly so good, and while he talked the older man would shake his head sadly and mutter to himself, 'He doesn't know, he doesn't know'.

The only thing to do was to deal with them separately, so I first of all sent the older man out of the room and got all the information I could out of the younger one, and then I got rid of him and I had the old man of 85 sitting there. And I asked him specific questions—points that I didn't know. I said, 'Now if you were going from this particular point in the mountains through the foothills to the plain what would the track be like?'

And he proceeded to give it me in the utmost detail. 'Four-hundred yards from that little turning, you step over a tiny stream—it's only about 4 feet wide—and then you turn to the left round some big boulders, etc. etc.'—it was a marvellous report he gave—and he said, 'Finally you come down into the plain and, of course, there is nothing more to be said—you are in the plain.' (Of course he was talking French, by the way.) 'Yes, you are in the plain, and it is all perfectly flat except (and then he began to smile) that a mile on there is one little hill which I think would interest you, because I understand you are an Archaeologist and I think its one of those artificial hills which cover an ancient site. It's quite small and not very high, but from the top of it you get a beautiful view of Adana lying away to the West.' All of a sudden his face changed. He sat forward in the chair and he said, 'From the top of that hill with one battery of guns you can knock Adana to Hell in half an hour'. I looked around and I saw, not an old man with a long white beard and bleary eyes, but a young vigorous-looking fellow.

I said, 'Father, what do you know about guns?'

And then there was a long silence and he leaned back in his chair and said, 'I commanded the French Artillery at the battle of Sedan when we surrendered to the Germans and that is why I am a Trappist monk'. And his voice had changed again and he was a weary old man of 85. It was one of the most sad things I have ever seen in my life. That sort of thing did happen.

Anyway, it made one's time in the office in Port Said extraordinarily interesting; and then that came to an end because I put out to sea. I'd got a nice little steam yacht, which belonged to Lord Rosebery really, called the Zaida, which I used for landing spies on the enemy coast and taking them off again. I was not feeling particularly well, and the Chief of Staff in Cairo said, 'Look here Woolley, next time the Zaida goes out to sea, you go on board'.

I objected, 'I can't spare the time'.

He said, 'Nonsense, you've got to take a holiday, it'll do you any amount of good, that's an order'.

So I said, 'All right', and the next time the Zaida put out to sea I went on it. We did a few jobs and then we put into the Gulf of Alexandretta, and we were having breakfast in the little deckhouse which was lit by skylights above and as it was hot weather the skylights were all wide open. We were just finishing breakfast; in fact the Captain had got up and walked to the door to go on the bridge to take his turn of duty, and the First Officer had just come in when there was a dull thud and the whole place went dark and deep green sea water came pouring down through the skylight.

The Captain, who had his hand on the door to open it, found he couldn't, and he turned round and said, 'Hm, they've got us this time'.

I saw the First Officer jump on to the table and dive upwards through the cascade of water that was coming through the skylight. It got light, the door opened, the Captain went out followed by myself, and the yacht was in two pieces, broken right in half, tilted right up and the ends going down. The Captain gave the order for everybody to jump overboard, and we did, and tried to swim away from the sinking ship, which went down. From the time we hit the mine it took exactly 28 seconds for the whole ship to disappear except for the mast which was still above water.

Well, we got away and the only bit of wreckage of any

size was the roof of the charthouse, which was a fair-sized square of matchboarding which floated on the surface but wouldn't have supported anybody. The Captain called out that everybody who could was to collect round that square. I may say that floating about everywhere there was no other wood to speak of, but there were life belts and things which had been loose on the deck, as would happen in wartime; they were drifting around, and we collected a lot of them, but there was a strong current and you couldn't possibly swim to the shore, which was about 3 miles off.

The Captain said, 'All right, everyone is to collect round the square and hold on. We're all going to die, so we may as well all go together.'

So we collected round it, and we'd got about sixteen people holding on to it with their heads just above water when suddenly some of the men began to laugh and one of them nudged me and said, 'Look over there, Sir'. I looked back and I saw two legs above water kicking violently in the air and then a moment later the legs went down and there came up a purple face with mouth open gasping for breath and I said, 'Good Heavens, it's the Cook'. And then the face disappeared and the legs came up again and I realised what had happened. The poor Cook had seized the lifebelt and put his feet through it with the result that he floated the wrong way up. So I swam up to him and put the lifebelt right and brought him along to our sort of raft.

I wanted to encourage him so I said to him, 'Well Cook, we've seen the last of the Zaida'.

He shook his head. (He was a big fat man, he'd been Lord Rosebery's Cook on the yacht.) And he said, 'It's terrible, Sir, that it should have happened today of all days'.

'Today of all days,' said I, 'Why? I don't see that it much matters whether we die yesterday, today or tomorrow.'

'Oh, yes,' he said, 'I wouldn't have minded tomorrow.'

'Why not?'

'Well, Sir, I don't know whether you remember, but the last time we left Port Said you were telling me of a way fellows have out here of cooking a goose with a stuffing of

dried peaches and the pistachio nuts and I was going to give
you that for dinner tonight, and I was coming to you after
breakfast, Sir, to find out exactly how that stuffing ought to

Cooking a goose

be made, and now the Zaida has gone and the goose has
gone and I shall never make that dish.'

I felt the real spirit of the artist was there: the chef could
be supremely indifferent to life or death as long as the goose
was cooked in the right way.

It was quite an extraordinary experience. We floated
there, hour after hour, expecting any moment to go down.
Nothing seemed to happen, we drifted slowly along in the
current and presently one of the men climbed up on to the
deckhouse roof, which promptly went down and we all got
a ducking and came up struggling.

The Captain, seeing what had happened—of course, the
man was still half sliding off the roof which was at an angle
—said, 'Johnson, get off that at once'.

And the stoker said, 'I'm tired, Sir, I don't see why I
shouldn't try to save my life'.

The Captain said, 'Stoker Johnson, if I have any lack of
discipline on board this ship I shall hold your head under
water'.

And the whole lot burst into shouts of laughter, though they all thought they were going to die.

Years after—well, I was a prisoner of war for 2½ years and it was after I got out—I told that story in the officers' cabin of a French man-of-war. I thought it was an amusing story so I repeated it, but I looked round and I saw very solemn faces. Two men had tears in their eyes, and then one said, 'Well, if we have another war perhaps at the end of it our Navy will come up to that standard'.

It was the idea of discipline of that sort—I mean, it was comic if you like, but it was the spirit of discipline that made the Navy what it is, and it was exhibited in that particular way. One likes to think that discipline is a quality of the English.

THE END

GEORGE ALLEN & UNWIN LTD
London : 40 Museum Street, W.C.1

Auckland : 24 Wyndham Street
Bombay : 15 Graham Road, Ballard Estate, Bombay 1
Buenos Aires : Escritorio 454-459, Florida 165
Calcutta : 17 Chittaranjan Avenue, Calcutta 13
Cape Town : 109 Long Street
Hong Kong : F1/12 Mirador Mansions, Kowloon
Karachi : Karachi Chambers, McLeod Road
Madras : Mohan Mansion, 38c Mount Road, Madras 6
Mexico : Villalongin 32-10, Piso, Mexico 5, D.F.
New Delhi : 13-14 Ajmeri Gate Extension, New Delhi 1
Sao Paulo : Avenida 9 de Julho, 1138-Ap. 51
Singapore : 36c Prinsep Street, Singapore 7
Sydney, N.S.W. : Bradbury House, 55 York Street
Toronto : 91 Wellington Street West

3. DAILY LIFE IN PERU

Under the Last Incas

LOUIS BAUDIN

The Inca Empire that was long established in Peru prior to its discovery by the Spanish conquistadors is one of the most astonishing pieces of racial organization the world has ever seen. Through the eyes of a man of the twentieth century, daily life in the times of the last Incas gives the impression of having been organized once and for all as a piece of mechanism of sad but surprising perfection. The absolute and the permanent reigned without opposition. The common people had nothing to learn, nothing to foresee, nothing to desire. They knew, to the last detail, what would be their lives from birth to death. There was for them no inner withdrawal, no outer radiance. The Inca Council, and they alone, constituted the brains of this immense collective personality.

Such the Empire appears to us: gigantic, yet with everything localized, a grandiose moment of time which repeated itself identically, a dream come true of an endless immensity and of duration without end.

However, the fourteenth-century Indian drew certain advantages from the situation. He owed to it an orderliness, a security against famine and invasion, peace of mind, a settlement into total passivity. And there were certain aspects of real grandeur: the splendours and riches of the imperial court, the astonishing architecture, the splendid pottery and textiles and public festivals, the unparalleled communications system, the wealth and military might.

Louis Baudin, a world authority on the subject, reconstitutes with great vividness every aspect of public and private life in a vast empire unknown to the old world and near its end. How did the people spend their days? How did they work? What did they eat, how did they play, how were they born and how did they die? What were their clothes like, what were the degrees of society, what were their tools, what were their dwellings like, what was their religion? The answers to all these questions, among many others, are here.

Illustrated. Demy 8vo. About 25s net

7. DAILY LIFE IN CHINA

On the Eve of the Mongol Invasion 1250-1276

JAQUES GERMET

Owing to China's vast area and long history, a particular time and place have been chosen for this description of daily life there.

The time is the period preceding the Mongol invasion, the last years of the Southern Sung dynasty, which, after the northern provinces had been lost to barbarian nomads from the steppes, ruled over South China only. This was a time when an astonishing development of large-scale commerce, with its accompanying extremes of exotically luxurious living and direst poverty, had made China the most advanced country in the world.

The place is Hangchow, the Southern Sung capital, later known to Marco Polo as Quinsai, and described by him as 'the most noble city and the best that is in the world'.

Mainly based on contemporary Chinese sources, a lively account is given here of the city—its streets, canals, markets and buildings—and of the people, of all sorts and conditions, who lived in it, the occupations they pursued, the pleasures they enjoyed, the clothes they wore, the food they ate, their social and civic life, their ceremonial occasions, their art and literature.

A picture emerges which is not only contemporary to the times it portrays, but also often gives the impression of being contemporary with certain aspects of our own times as well.

Demy 8vo. Illustrated. About 30s net

8. DAILY LIFE IN ITALY

in the 18th Century

forthcoming title

MAURICE VAUSSARD

GEORGE ALLEN & UNWIN LTD